ECHOES OF MEMORY

KIPRONO MUTAI

Published by Spines
ISBN: 979-8-89383-511-3

CONTENTS

This book is dedicated to my parents, the late Senior Pastor Joseph Chepkwony and Mama Grace. Their unwavering efforts and hard work have been the foundation of my life, and their dedication will never go unrecognized. Both of them labored tirelessly, instilling in me and my siblings the values of perseverance, integrity, and faith. Pastor Joseph's spiritual guidance and Mama Grace's nurturing care provided solid ground for us to grow and thrive. Their sacrifices and steadfast commitment have shaped us into the successful adults we are today, and this book stands as a testament to their enduring love and remarkable legacy.

ABOUT THE AUTHOR

I was born in 1986 in a tiny village called Kiptogoch, where it's easy to spot a stranger because everyone knows each other. With a population of about 5,000, the village boasts a strong sense of community, where people care for one another during times of need. The name Kiptogoch, meaning "face" in the Kipsigis language, likely refers to the visage of a creature, although no one ever specified its true meaning, and I never thought to investigate further. Situated in Bomet District in the Great Rift Valley, Kiptogoch is part of one of Kenya's historic regions, rich in culture and heritage.

Back in the days, especially in the 80s, and even today, people often described their homes by pointing out directions, naming close neighbours, or referencing nearby public buildings such as schools and churches to provide a clue to their location. It was common practice to use familiar landmarks to guide visitors, making the directions more personal and relatable. Some would go a step further, offering a perfect geographical description that included natural features like hills, distinctive trees, and bushes as cues. This method painted a vivid picture of the surroundings, helping anyone unfamiliar with the area to navigate with ease. The use of these tangible and familiar markers created a sense of community and connection, embedding the location within the shared experiences and landscape of the area.

Every child born in the *Kipsigis* community is given a name based on the time of birth and it is usually done by mothers with the help of midwives or close relatives present during birth. I came to realise later on as I grew up that my name was a symbol of early morning around five o'clock in the evening. You would imagine that nearly every other newborn of the same gender born around that same time in my community would bear the same name based on that naming system.

I am the fifth born, and this didn't mean anything because all my siblings were treated equally except for the last born who breastfed until around preschool age. We made fun of him up to date. I am sure he would dismiss the accusation; we love him, and we still pick on him, but not when his kids are around. He finally decided to give up breastfeeding when we started making fun of him and threatening to tell him off at school. Such a threat was to be taken seriously because there were standby bullies who would take the matter to another level. Sooner or later, the whole school would know about the action. It was a common bullying exercise that was not punishable.

Growing up in my community, all the children, including myself, learned the Kipsigis language and embraced our rich cultural heritage. As a young boy, I was taught to perform the essential duties expected of every man, such as looking after domestic animals, fencing, farming, and spending time with grown men to learn how to talk and behave like them. Above all, I learned to respect parents and adults, regardless of their status. This period was filled with lessons on good behaviour, the difference between right and wrong, and the importance of helping out around the homestead. I also gained knowledge in environmental science, particularly the significance of planting trees. My father was an excellent teacher at that age, always emphasising the importance of maintaining a clean and green environment. He would often say, "Every time you cut a tree, plant two," instilling in us a lifelong respect for nature.

In this community that I grew up in, at the age of two, all kids are able to speak their "mother tongue" fluently. This first language was named as such because kids spend most of their time with their mothers learning. You can tell one of the responsibilities of mothers is to teach their kids how to speak. Most children who were not able to speak fluently by a certain age would have their mothers looked down upon for not being able to teach their kids. I was lucky because I was one of the beneficiaries of that mutual relationship with my mother. I had nearly mastered all the vocabulary by the age of three. Everything else was perfected at early school age since it was in the school curriculum. The lesson was called vernacular; it often included learning the names of the months, seasons, great leaders, and all other important cultural history and events.

Kiprono Mutai, MPH

1

Being born in a small village up in the country was the norm, a big issue for some people, but nobody knew that success would come upon some, if not most, of the kids born and raised in a village. Children raised in a rural area like this were always considered primitive, poor, and often nothing compared to children brought up in urban centres, which were considered richer and more educated. My own understanding was that you grow up, go to a local school, maybe join a high school in the village, and later on go back to provide free labor on the farm owned by parents.

The well-known family vehicle was a two-wheel Road Master bicycle, 21 inches to be precise, crucial for getting around. My father, with his remarkable strength, could ride as far as the small city of Sotik, a distance of about 30 miles round trip. The ride on our two-wheeler was unforgettable and truly special. Even during my high school years, I would ride with my father, taking turns peddling. While some might have thought it was silly, they were missing out on a unique bonding experience. These rides provided us with precious opportunities to connect and talk about life, making them cherished memories that I hold dear. He would take off in the morning and pedal his way to cash in his monthly earnings at Barclays Bank, one of the largest banks at that time. From the moment he left home, we eagerly awaited his return, curious about what he would bring back. Our greatest hope was for bread and a kilogram of meat, usually fresh intestines, which my mother, with her exceptional cooking skills, would prepare into a delicious meal. As my father rolled into the compound, he would ring the bicycle bell, signalling his return. We would run out as fast as our tiny legs could carry us to welcome him, eyes fixed on the shopping bag, guessing its contents. He never disappointed, always bringing home some goodies. The next day, knowing there was cash in the house, we maintained exemplary behaviour, hoping he would send us to the local canteen to buy necessities. This strategy allowed us to keep the change, a wish that was always granted and always paid off.

In most cases, it was true, which made the belief hard to challenge because it was the cycle of life. In a village in my situation, especially in those early years or in the 90s, it was a place easy to identify kids' gender because most of them, especially boys, would walk around the homestead with either thorn shorts, no shirt, or at the extreme, naked. To justify their actions, they always said that they were waiting for their clothes to dry out in the sun. The level of poverty in those years was high, but as young children, we never noticed because we always had food to fill our bellies and never lacked homemade toys to play with. Thinking about the past at my current age, you would walk around the neighbourhood and all you see is pretty much nothing except hungry but healthy chickens, sometimes malnourished cats, stray dogs, cows grazing, cow dung everywhere, and sometimes a urine smell around the compound where the boys lived. As kids, we spent most of the time playing with our friends outside and would only come back when it was mealtimes.

Laundry time was unforgettable, a weekend ritual especially on Sunday mornings at the river owned by my uncle Joel. Everyone did their laundry at the same time, turning it into a communal meeting ground. The river source was fresh and clean, with separate areas for drinking, cows, and washing. My older sisters were tasked with the laundry, and they always delivered five-star service, leaving our clothes spotless and smelling fresh. As young boys, we often tried to accompany them, but it was strictly prohibited because the same river was used for bathing. In minutes, the young women from around the village would turn the river into a communal shower with zero privacy. This was not a scene from a movie but a real-life occurrence, and it was for our own good not to be present. Age restrictions were enforced, but the shorter boys, often mistaken for younger than their age, never kept the secret and would give us vivid, precise descriptions of the scene. These boys were so gifted, they never missed any detail.

In the village, kids learn by example, good or bad. They learn to be teachers, doctors, pilots, drivers, artists, and even thugs and what have you. We learned to imitate everything. We learned how to curse, gamble, swear, and mostly to fight, especially boys. As a young boy, you would not want to be whipped by a girl around your age; it would bring you shame and a very bad day for you and risk losing friends. As young as two, some kids were able to swear, utter curses including wishing lightning would come down and strike somebody and many others. A common curse was calling upon Anthrax on somebody—at that young age. By then, I didn't even know what Anthrax was until one of our cows died from the disease; it was terrible because the carcass had to be burned before burying to make sure the virus was completely eradicated.

Despite all the norms and beliefs, my father had always overseen hope and a better life in the future. He was a man of his own words, and he believed in hard work. A typical village man would say that he was the first man to transform a thatched roof hut into an iron sheet and moved the family from owning a goat to several cows. If you grew up in the villages of Africa or at least have read stories and visited some of the remote places in Kenya, you would agree with that statement.

Boys or young men were groomed and taught better ways to take care of themselves, and a common practice was taking communal showers together in the river. This time was also used for socialising and comparing the size of our manhood, with the smallest often earning a nickname unless a bribe was offered to keep it quiet, promising to improve the diet, particularly by eating more eggs, to catch up with the rest of the group. As we grew older, this practice became a habit, eventually gaining approval from the older boys and even the parents.

Everything was fun; from running to school every morning without shoes to swimming in the river with dangerous wild animals. We hunted birds with homemade bows and arrows and chased stray dogs, all at a young age. Safety always came last; danger was the least of our concerns. For instance, my older brother would shoot an arrow into the sky and ask us to wait and see where it landed, a situation that always ended in a narrow escape. Despite the risks, these adventures were the highlights of our childhood, filled with excitement and camaraderie.

We knew a lot about first aid without being taught; it was by heart. I witnessed one of my close relatives by the name *Jogoo* falling down, hitting a rock down in the river and ending up with arterial bleeding. While some of us kids were busy running to find rescue, my older brother was busy applying pressure to stop the bleeding and calming the boy down, saving his life. The situation was under control, and no one ended up in the hospital, and parents did not even know what happened that day. Instead, the accident was reported as a minor scratch. Another incident was when my cousin, *Kiplangat Bor* fell off a swing, hitting his spine really hard, ending up with an altered mental status in seconds, rolling his eyes around and passing out. Quick reaction was to massage his spine and in seconds, he was back to normal. That was another high-level type of first aid. The last one is when I jumped over a live fence after a few of my friends successfully jumped; it happened that I barely made it over to the other side of the fence, fell down landing my left hand on a three-inch thorn that went through the palm of my wrist. My older brother pulled it out and told me to spit on it and apply pressure at the same time, keep moving so as to get to fishing just in time. My wrist was back in business the next day with zero hospitalisation, and my parents did not even have a clue what had happened.

I grew up in this evergreen village with no life-threatening weather, gangsters, or wild animals like what most people would imagine. Gun violence was only known from movies and real stories shared by heroes like Ezekiel, who was deployed to Yugoslavia for peacekeeping. I admired it; people lived closely, and shared similarities and they always came together to share common problems such as death in the neighbourhood or the arrival of a newborn baby and initiation ceremonies. Families who lacked basic necessities such as milk, flour, and kerosene for their lanterns would visit the nearest neighboring house to borrow and return the same favor later on or simply exchange something. If you missed out on growing up in a village, to my knowledge, this means you can run to your next door to borrow some brown sugar when you have guests for your tea. It was always guaranteed when you quoted the word guests to come in unexpectedly.

I miss the harvesting seasons; this was a time when other families sought help harvesting corn and at times during planting seasons too and later on, we would also go asking for help in return. I grew up learning the importance of team-work. I have six siblings named Agnes, Jesca, Erick, Zeddy, Ben, and John and I am the fifth. You would think it is a big family, but this is a typical average family during those early years when the economy was still good, and the cost of life was cheap. Currently, the economy is not suitable for such big families anymore because basic needs have become expensive and sources of income do not yield proportionally to the size of the family, but yield based on hard work and effort from the head of the house, usually the father.

Even though the economy was still good, necessities food such as bread, meat, cooking oil and other nutritious foods were hardly eaten. Maybe chicken once in a while because my sisters kept a number of them.

Televisions and radios were hardly seen around here, and even if there was one, you would get in trouble for going close to it, not to mention trying to operate it. And the main reason for this kind of restriction was the fear of the cost of repair in case of damage and only if you were lucky to find someone to fix it. We knew of one old man by the name *Arap Mibei* who was well known for repairing electronics; according to my judgment and what others said about him, he never went to any school, but he seemed to understand most of the laws of physics which some of us don't and it always amazes me. Every time we took a broken radio to his shop, he would look at it, listen, tap and tell you what is wrong with it and estimate the time of cost and repair. One major problem with his customers including us was payment. Most of the payment for his services was always at a later time; sometimes this was met but mostly never. For some situations, he was forced to lock up your electronic devices until payment is made or whenever you go in as a returning customer with another broken device, he reminds you of outstanding balances forcing you to pay the balances before starting the new service.

We got used to the strict rules and we didn't care very much, and the only way we would go near any kind of electronic was when no one was around, but still, my younger brother would likely tell on me anytime whenever I didn't do him a favor. I came to realize later that it was the best way to learn what was right and wrong. Birthdays were never celebrated; it wasn't a big thing, and you won't even remember when your birthday arrived; I had it written somewhere but it always passed. I had a memorable childhood. I was always happy, playful and never cared about so many things as long as Christmas and other public holidays such as New Years were celebrated. A pair of new clothes, perhaps, a Christmas selection and a pair of school uniforms every other January was all I needed.

You might have missed the most fun part of childhood. Riding on a bicycle as a means of transportation with my father was the best especially on a paved road. This was the best chance to hear stories of day-to-day life and get to meet his friends in town and get a chance to drink a soda and a piece of bread and bring home a piece to the rest of the family. Life was extremely good. He was one of the most well-known people owning a Road Master, one framed, 24-inch bicycle, well taken care of and always in good condition. Mondays, Tuesdays, Thursdays, and Fridays were well-known market days, and we took turns once in a while to go shopping for one another, but it was always more fun to go with a sister because they were the ones who really knew how to shop for the best outfits. I was well known for picking up outfits twice my size with a good reason of growing up with them, but the clothes would always get worn out before I grew enough to fit in them. As kids, shoes were highly in demand; we liked them and we felt so special to wear them, wash them, and wake up every morning double-checking to make sure it was still there the next day.

Being brought up in a non-Christian family, we admired children from other families who attended Sunday schools, attended Vocational Bible Schools, learned memory verses in English, Bible stories, sang and got presents for attending. Even though my parents never attended church by then, still they would encourage us to attend Sunday schools under one condition that me and my two younger brothers would line up to be showered with ice-cold water in the morning. We liked fighting during shower time, but my dad was around with a piece of stick in position to whip any one of us who would try to put up a fight. Most of the fighting was to make sure you always get a bath last, so that next time you won't do the same thing. We encountered well-known bullies outside our home who would block the road and threaten to beat us up or throw mud at us, call you names unless you either bribe them with a banana or baked corn to get across the road or get a cover-up with another adult if you were lucky to see one going the same direction. You won't want to get into a fight with them because there were a lot of them and once you get into a fight, the fight will go on and will be carried forward to school and other public places and will probably get you into trouble with the parents for fighting. We had a few families in the village who were good at making bullies. We knew them and no one would do anything about them. They only got over it with age.

The village is a good example of a male chauvinistic society. In most cases, if not nearly all, men are in charge. Regardless of what needs to be done, it has to be done as long as the man in the house okays it. We were lucky our father was not a drunkard like the others, because some families would have the head of the house giving tasks to be completed and taking off to drink. Return in the evening looking like a chicken with its head cut off, fighting the mother who has been working all day to feed the family. We would always know when there was a fight in the neighbourhood or across the valley; a good sign would be some loud bang of utensils, a few complaints of not well-cooked food and screams followed by a run around the house, a man trying to catch the wife to punish. What the heck? As kids, we never admired such people, and my dad would always call them names he never wanted us to tell anyone. Daily life in the village has always been the same; most of the people including my family work on the tea farm every other day. If it was not picking tea, it would be weeding, planting, or even feeding farm animals. These daily tasks become a routine and lifestyle of the society, and simply by the landscape of the area, you would distinguish the hard-working families from the lazy ones.

At this stage, only big cities like Nairobi, the capital of

Kenya, only existed in a dream. To our standards, only rich and educated people with jobs who speak English and Swahili would go. Even though I had vivid memories of the existence of such a big town, I admired being associated with city people and especially the broadcasters who we assumed to be in the city even if they broadcast on a local radio station in other small cities. I admired some people in the neighbourhood listening to English radio stations; I could not fully understand, but I would pay close attention just to pick up a few words in English and use them around even if it did not fit whatever I was expressing. I remember the common English words such as "in fact", and "as a matter of fact" was in my dictionary and I would put it out there to scare some bullies off and to impress the right people especially teachers in school.

2

Growing up in the Rift Valley of Kenya, a region renowned for its fertile land and conducive farming environment, was a unique and enriching experience. The Rift Valley, with its well-known reputation for farming cash crops like tea and various food crops, as well as dairy farming, shaped not only my family's livelihood but also the way of life for many in my village. Farming has been a tradition carried over for generations, and land ownership is deeply intertwined with individual wealth and wellness. The larger the land, the wealthier the family is perceived to be, which often holds true.

My father dedicated his life to tea farming, a practice that was introduced to our region in the early 1980s. It wasn't until the 1990s that the local market began to flourish, prompting many to recognise the benefits of tea plantations. Watching my parents work diligently on the farm, I came to see farming as a way of life, a sentiment shared by many in our region. For my parents, farming was more than just an occupation; it was a blessing that brought success and prosperity, enabling them to invest in our education. Their unwavering dedication and hard work on the farm provided the foundation for our family's well-being and future opportunities.

Life in the Rift Valley revolves around farming, with nearly every Kenyan from this region having stories of earning a living through tea farming, cattle rearing, and other agricultural activities. Basic commodities like milk, corn, and beans are essential to daily life, and their absence signifies disaster and hunger. Milk, in particular, holds a crucial role—not only as a staple for family consumption but also as a vital source of income. Surplus milk is sold to neighbours or the local cooperative creameries, providing financial support to many households. The rhythm of life in the Rift Valley is deeply intertwined with these agricultural practices, shaping the community's identity and sustenance.

During my childhood in the early 1990s, the Kenya Cooperative Creameries (K.C.C.) was the main buyer of milk from farmers. My mother would wake up early to milk the cows, prepare the milk, and transport it to a local collection centre. My father or older siblings would then take the milk to the centre for collection by a K.C.C. lorry. This system worked well until the company's collapse due to poor management, which devastated many farmers, including my family, who lost months of unpaid milk supplies. The collapse of Kenya Cooperative Creameries (K.C.C) brought a wave of despair and anguish to farmers who had long relied on it as their lifeline. The once-thriving cooperative, which had provided a stable market and fair prices for their milk, suddenly ceased to exist, leaving farmers in a lurch. The pain was palpable; many felt betrayed and abandoned, their hard work seemingly for nothing. Families who had depended on the steady income from dairying faced financial uncertainty and hardship. The sight of milk being poured away or sold at a pittance to opportunistic middlemen was heartbreaking. The collapse not only impacted their livelihoods but also shattered their trust in cooperative institutions, leaving a lingering sense of loss and insecurity in the farming community.

This period marked a turning point in my life. Witnessing my father's investments go unpaid and the subsequent hardships made me acutely aware of the importance of education. As a response, my family, along with other villagers, shifted their focus to tea farming, which proved to be more reliable and rewarding. The annual tea bonus provided a significant financial boost, often coinciding with Christmas, creating visible differences in families' wealth based on their tea earnings. This shift not only stabilised our economic situation but also reinforced the value of hard work and strategic planning, underscoring the critical role that education and sustainable farming played in securing a better future for our community.

December in the Rift Valley is not just a festive season; it is a time steeped in tradition and significance, particularly marked by circumcision ceremonies among the Kalenjin community. For me, undergoing this ritual at the age of fourteen was a profound rite of passage, signifying my transition from childhood to adulthood. I went through the circumcision ritual along with 13 other agemates—Matthew, Martin, Benard, Timothy, Nickson, Erick, Kosgei, the late Solomon, Benard from *Kamobiriri*, Enock, Anyenyo, Walter, and Leonard—marking a significant transition in our lives. All of us belong to Kaplelach, one of the eight age sets of the Kalenjin people. During this period, we were separated from our families for about a month. The family of Mr. and Mrs. Koech generously took care of all of us, providing not only shelter and nourishment but also invaluable mentorship. They guided us through this important journey of becoming men, instilling in us the responsibilities and values we would need in our adult lives. We spent most of our time reading, learning, and absorbing the wisdom shared by our mentors, which prepared us for the responsibilities and challenges that lay ahead. This period was not just about the physical ritual but also about growing mentally and emotionally, thanks to the unwavering support and guidance of the Koech family.

This pivotal moment was not just about the physical act but also about the deeper cultural lessons that accompanied it. I began to understand the concept of age sets, the camaraderie and shared responsibilities that come with it, and the paramount importance of respecting elders. This period instilled in me a newfound maturity and a serious attitude towards my education and future endeavours. The values and discipline I embraced during this time have been instrumental in shaping my journey, driving me to achieve my goals and honour the traditions that laid the foundation for my character and success.

December is generally a festive season often marked by feasting, celebrations, and drinking. If this month finds you broke, it's considered a bad year for you and your family. Children take pride in boasting about how much rice and wheat flour their families have bought for the season. For fathers, it can be deeply disappointing to return home empty-handed during this time. The pressure to provide can lead some to cope by drinking, trying to avoid the inevitable questions about their financial struggles. The festive atmosphere only heightens the sense of failure and frustration, making the contrast between those who can afford to celebrate lavishly and those who cannot even more stark.

Walking away from other families during mealtimes,

knowing you were going home to a meal of collard greens or traditional vegetables like black nightshade, was challenging. These vegetables, though highly nutritious, were often a last resort when food supplies were low. The sight and aroma of rich meals in other homes highlighted the humble fare awaiting you, making the walk home a bittersweet experience. It's believed that our ancestors discovered these hardy greens through necessity and experimentation, learning to appreciate their health benefits despite their association with scarcity. This knowledge was passed down through generations, turning these humble plants into a symbol of resilience and resourcefulness, even as they reminded us of lean times.

Village life is characterised by a strong sense of community, where the bonds between neighbours are deep and enduring. Villagers come together to settle conflicts, celebrate ceremonies, and support one another in times of need, creating a tightly knit fabric of mutual aid and understanding. Fundraising for school fees is a common practice, reflecting their collective commitment to education and the future of their children. Similarly, community support during sad events like deaths ensures that no family bears the burden alone. Christianity plays a significant role in daily life, with Sundays revered as a holy day dedicated to worship and rest. This religious influence fosters good morals and a profound sense of unity, guiding the villagers in their interactions and reinforcing the shared values that hold the community together.

Funerals in the rural village of *Kiptogoch* are profound moments of communal mourning and solidarity. When a loved one passes away, the entire village comes together to grieve and offer support, reflecting the deep bonds that unite them. Family, friends, and neighbours gather at the deceased's home, where a canopy is often erected to provide shelter for the mourners. The air is filled with somber hymns and prayers, as villagers lend their voices to the collective sorrow and hope for comfort. Women prepare meals and serve tea, ensuring that everyone is nourished during these trying times, while men arrange the logistics of the burial. Contributions are collected to ease the financial burden on the bereaved family, demonstrating the community's unwavering support. As the funeral procession moves towards the burial site, there is a shared sense of loss and reverence, but also of unity and love. The prayers and eulogies highlight the life of the departed, celebrating their contributions and the memories they leave behind. In *Kiptogoch*, funerals are not just about saying goodbye; they are about coming together to mourn, to remember, and to uphold the enduring spirit of community and care.

Religion is a cornerstone of life in the village, deeply woven into the fabric of the community. From a young age, children are introduced to the practice of attending church, where they join their families in singing hymns and offering prayers. Each Sunday, the village becomes a mosaic of devotion, with families making their way to various churches, their spirits lifted by the collective worship. These gatherings are more than just religious observances; they are a vital part of the village's cultural heritage, passed down from generation to generation. The teachings and values imparted during these services instill a sense of morality, compassion, and unity among the villagers. Church activities, including Sunday school, choir practice, and community outreach, foster a sense of belonging and reinforce the importance of faith in daily life. This enduring tradition ensures that the spiritual bonds remain strong, guiding the community through life's challenges and celebrations with a shared sense of purpose and hope.

Despite the prevalent religious beliefs, drinking among adults was and remains a common practice. We admired the drinkers for their comedic gifts in social settings, and through them, we learned that alcohol is a chemical that alters the human brain. We witnessed drunkards performing what seemed like miracles in the streets, engaging in fights and cursing each other in scenes that, if captured today, would undoubtedly go viral on TikTok. We saw alcohol transform individuals into perfect English speakers, a phenomenon we couldn't quite explain. In some cases, we saw wives being chased off the homestead, only to return the next day when their husbands sobered up and demanded their return. This behaviour was never questioned, not even by the local chief. There were no grudges, and the wives would not dare to ask their husbands why they were chased out. Remaining quiet was the easiest way to make peace and ensure the family's prosperity.

3

Kenya uses the 8-4-4 British system of education. I liked this education system and its community-based setting because most kids were either from the same family or related in one way or another. I remember admiring my older siblings every morning as they got ready to go to school, while I stayed home to help with simple chores such as looking after the cows and making sure they got water at certain times of the day. Recently, under the leadership of former President Uhuru Kenyatta, the Kenyan Competence-Based Curriculum (CBC) was introduced. The CBC is a new system of education designed by the Kenya Institute of Curriculum Development (KICD) team and launched by the Ministry of Education in 2017. At the end of the learning period, the learner should have been molded to have the following values: love, responsibility, respect, unity, peace, patriotism, integrity, self-efficacy, and digital literacy.

Seeing *Tila* join junior high school at a young age at Tenwek Junior High was both inspiring and a cause for concern.

The Competency-Based Curriculum (CBC) had paved the way for his early enrollment, a testament to his academic prowess and the changing educational landscape. As he stood by the gate with his suitcase, ready to embark on this new chapter, his youthful face mirrored a blend of excitement and apprehension. The suitcase seemed almost too large for his small frame, symbolizing the weight of expectations and the journey ahead. His determination was palpable, inspiring those around him who saw in him the promise of a bright future. Yet, there was a shared concern among onlookers about the challenges he might face, both academically and socially, given his tender age. The sight of *Tila* bravely stepping into this new world captured the essence of the CBC's potential to nurture young talent, while also highlighting the community's hope and collective prayers for his success and well-being.

Our beautiful mud home was directly across from one of the main local schools, perched up in the hills. From our vantage point, we could see the older students in their uniforms bustling about during breaks, their voices carried across the distance as they played, screamed, and sometimes sang during P.E. lessons. The lively scene filled us with anticipation, making us eagerly await our elder siblings' return to hear about the day's events. They would share stories from their classes, especially if someone got into trouble, adding a layer of excitement to our evenings. On days when it involved a different grade, our siblings might not have the details, but their animated recaps of their own experiences kept us enthralled and connected to the vibrant world just across the way.

Jesca, my second-born sister, was renowned in our village for her captivating storytelling, weaving tales that left everyone enthralled and eager for more. Her hospitality was equally legendary; she had an innate ability to make everyone feel at home, always ensuring guests were well-fed and comfortable. However, Jesca was also known for her fiery temper and swift punitive actions when provoked, a testament to her fierce spirit and strong sense of justice. One harrowing day, her life was almost cut short when she fell gravely ill. The lack of emergency services in our village turned a dire situation into a near tragedy, as we struggled to get her the urgent medical care she needed. The memory of that day is a stark reminder of the vulnerabilities we faced, highlighting the preciousness of Jesca's resilience and the deep bonds of family and community that ultimately helped her pull through.

When it was time for me to start school, I was finally admitted to a nursery school in the village, at a walking distance of less than a mile from home. This is the equivalent of a preschool in the modern Western education system. I started attending nursery school in 1991. The first day was so exciting, especially having met all the milestones and parent requirements to go to school. Going to school in those years meant getting a brand-new uniform, shoes if you were lucky, and school supplies, including a pencil with an eraser, and a ruled and squared book. Instead of a backpack, I had a homemade pouch that held my school stuff quite well. Homemade items weren't considered very cool; the ones made by a tailor were neater and more colorful, but who cared? They did the same job. The only time it failed was if there was an unfinished seam in one of the corners, and you would end up losing a pencil, sometimes more than once. To solve this, there were several options: getting yelled at for being careless, mending the tear, or cutting the pencil into three to four pieces to leave one at home as a spare and take the other to school. Life goes on.

School time was from 7:30 a.m. to 12:00 p.m., after which we would go home the next day. There were no snacks provided, but my mother always made sure I had some sort of snack packed for the day, which I would often trade or share with friends. Not every kid was able to bring food to school, and sometimes I was discouraged from taking food to school to toughen me up for "real" school, which was further away. I made friends with older kids who were generous enough to share their food. Popular snacks included roasted corn, which was not soft but hardened and ready to be harvested. Often barely roasted at 6:30 a.m., it wouldn't be accessed until break time at 10:00 a.m. Sneaky kids would constantly munch on it, often getting in trouble because the roasted corn smell was easy to trace back to the owner. The best punishment, which I thought was fair, was passing the corn around the class for everyone to get a taste, even that naughty kid you never liked. They would laugh as they threw the cob away. We loved it and couldn't wait to see who would get busted the next day.

I am surprised I never got busted. I never carried food to school; my parents didn't encourage it, and it was chaotic in the morning to roast corn while my mother made breakfast using the same fire pit. I stayed off the fireplace except to warm myself while waiting for breakfast.

The punishment of sharing the corn became common, leading to kids snitching on those sneaking food. Some took this advantage too far, stealing their desk matés' food and expecting the same justice. They were eventually caught and punished. The means of punishment were not corporal but included kneeling with hands raised high, which could last as long as the teacher wanted. If you lowered your hands, other kids would alert the teacher, resulting in further punishment for disobedience. This discipline was beneficial later in life, as most of the well-behaved kids excelled in nursery school and were promoted to first grade.

It is hard to imagine an elementary school without a latrine, but we didn't have one for almost a year. Instead, we were asked to use the bush for peeing, with boys on one side and girls on the other. Peeping on girls was highly discouraged and punished. Some shy kids would pee on themselves rather than ask for permission, and they were sent home for the day. Desk mates were asked to watch for them, but it was hard to catch them in the act.

Madam Joyce was the epitome of elegance and grace, always impeccably dressed and exuding a sense of calm and assurance. Her caring nature and sharp intellect made her a pillar of support for all of us. Despite being funded by our parents rather than the government, her dedication and expertise far exceeded any expectations. I spent about two transformative years under her care before being promoted to the first class. Madam Joyce was more than a teacher; she was like a perfect mother, providing a sense of security and warmth. One of the most memorable lessons she imparted was teaching us to sing in rounds, a joyful and unifying experience. My friends, including Robert, the strong and protective son of Maina, were a constant source of comfort, especially against bullies. The day Madam Joyce walked us to a larger primary school for enrolment in the first grade was unforgettable. I could hardly believe my eyes as I joined one of the biggest institutions for higher learning. Her absence left a void, and I deeply missed her hospitality and nurturing presence.

4

If you still remember the name of your first-grade teacher, you probably don't want to miss this story. First of all, my name changed from Johnston to Robert because my sister recommended a name change, feeling the other name didn't suit me for some reason. I took her recommendation; changing a name was as easy as breathing because you could just wake up one morning and tell people that your name had changed!

Baptism was also another way to change a name. You would tell the ordained pastor the new name you wanted to be baptised with, and from that moment, your name would change. So, I changed my name on the first day of enrolling in first grade. At first, when asked my name by the teacher, Moses, I stammered, "Johnston-Robert, no-no, Robert," insisting on the new name. He instantly knew I was transitioning to Robert and asked if I was changing my name, which I denied, claiming my previous name was my brother's. He understood but cared less, proceeding to write my new name down. Just like that, my name was formally changed once it was entered into the school attendance register. I was shy and thought I was in trouble until he asked me to sit down, and I felt relieved that the name change was successful.

A few of my old friends continued calling me by the old name, and the trick to stop them was to cry every time they did. Crying was magical in the '90s because it meant two things: whoever made you cry would get in trouble when your friends told the teacher, or you would win yourself a free snack as a bribe to not escalate the situation. It was magnificent. I remember one of the bullies making me cry, and everyone in the class surrounded me, asking if they were responsible for my tears. The rule was to keep saying no until the last one that didn't show up was the victim. The whole class would then go to him and ask for compensation, or else he would be forwarded for corporal punishment. It was my lucky day because my bribe turned out to be a 3.0-volt burnt-out bulb. It was a perfect gift, hard to find; common gifts were mostly electronics with wires, regardless of length or insulation.

The main primary school that served our community was about five miles from home, one of the largest in the district with over 500 pupils. Some classes were divided into three sections, but most, including mine, were split into two: Standard One East and West, while others were labeled North and South, Green, Yellow, and Blue. The teacher-to-pupil ratio was 1:35 or sometimes higher, especially in the middle and senior classes. All the classrooms were lively and full of noise, as making noise was a specialty for most kids. Perhaps this was because at home, strict rules kept our mouths shut, making the school a place where we could express ourselves freely.

Beginning in first grade, most classes were general, covering core subjects like English, Swahili, Math, and others like Science, Art and Crafts, Christian Religious Education (C.R.E), Home Science, and Music. We were also taught the vernacular as one of the lessons but were restricted on when to speak it to learn how to communicate in English and Kiswahili. Back then, English was harder to speak, and Swahili was emphasised the most. We did not know how to read initially but were required to know by third grade to be promoted to fourth grade, considered the upper class. Upper classes had subjects broken down, for example, Science became pure Science and Agriculture, and other subjects like Geography and History were introduced.

I struggled to read because my third-grade teacher, the late *Paulina Sawe*, liked me and, wanted the best for me. The late Paulina Sawe was a gifted elementary school teacher whose skills were destined to transform the lives of her students. Short, with dark skin, and always smelling pleasant, she was strict and the kind of teacher you wouldn't want to disappoint, especially when it came to reading or writing. Her genuine concern for my academic improvement led her to visit my home one afternoon. This visit was the best time of my life and marked the moment I realised she truly wanted the best for me. Her dedication and care made that visit unforgettable, forever impacting my perspective on education.

I never got a chance to sit at the back because I was among the shortest in class, and the sitting arrangements were height-based. One of the famous English textbooks was called "Read with Us." The book had short stories and discussion questions at the end. It was easier to understand and answer questions when the teacher read the book slowly, breaking the story down to our level. Later, she would go around the class asking random questions, and whoever got it wrong would be punished.

This motivated me to learn how to read by utilising my older siblings, who were then in seventh and eighth grade. They were very helpful, and every day I started reading some vocabulary that most of my classmates could not understand. The fun part was that when you knew how to read, you earned the opportunity to sit with others who knew how to read, while non-readers were singled out in a hot row of dummies. The first row was for the smart ones, the second row for the average, and the third row was for those who could not read, often noisy troublemakers. The teacher was kind enough to offer remedial classes for them, sometimes asking us to help. It felt good to read a whole paragraph in front of the class while others watched, salivating. As the term ended, those who couldn't read were retained for another year unless their parents intervened and demanded promotion to the next class.

Fourth grade was when my grades started dropping because math became more complex with double digits and lots of multiplication. I often found myself playing and sitting out in the sun instead of studying. I never liked the math teacher because he was known for his corporal punishment. He was known for his phrase, "Isn't that so?" A very smart teacher who had transferred from one of the best private schools in the region, *Kipkoi Junior Academy*. I dropped so low that I even scored zero on a class assignment. I never told anyone because it was shameful. Just imagine having a big zero out of ten question written in your math book almost every day. It got so bad that sometimes the teacher would annotate the word, "See me," on top of my exercise book. That phrase could ruin your entire day or even worse if it was a Friday, then your weekend would be ruined.

When I saw that phrase, I would find buddies in the same

boat, and one day, five of us decided to see him in the staff room. Big mistake. We ended up kneeling down, each getting at least four canes in the butt region. This teacher would grab your head, tuck you between his knees so you couldn't move, and whip you. If you were the last to get whipped, you would try to run away, seeing the serious canning going on. The only way out was to get the math right and keep moving as quitting was not an option.

My buddy, Reuben, was excellent at math, always scoring ten out of ten. He was not allowed to share answers, but sometimes I would sneak a peek and copy. The stupid part was that while the answers were right, the method of obtaining them was not legit, and I couldn't explain how I got them right. Not a smart move. Punishment changed from caning to ear pinching and pulling, getting worse, but quitting was still not an option. Robert's brother Mario was a team player who always coached me on dress codes to endure the pain during the caning process; his unique style of doubling or tripling pairs of shorts on math days taught me the importance of teamwork and resilience. I had to step up my game, putting more effort into and seeking assistance from my older sisters. The day multiplication made sense was towards the end of the school year when I was among the top four students who performed well.

A year passed quickly, and I survived the class. I managed to communicate with teachers in Swahili and occasionally in English, and my proficiency in other subjects balanced things out. Promoted to fifth grade, I began to improve in math, thanks to a teacher who liked me and helped me catch up on what I missed in fourth grade. Each day, I grew smarter, steadily rising to the top of the class. By the end of the term, my efforts were recognised, and I was acknowledged along with other pupils who excelled.

Another fourth-grade teacher, *Pricilla Tesot*, was well known for her captivating stories. Gentle and kind, she never resorted to canning anyone. Her favourite subject was home science, with a particular emphasis on hygiene. She was always dressed to impress, entering the classroom smelling wonderful and greeting us warmly. After efficiently covering the lesson in a few minutes, she would spend the rest of the time motivating us to work hard and aim for studying abroad. Her storytelling gift was epic, especially her vivid descriptions of a flight to China, which left me in awe. She recounted a breathtaking yet scary tale of how one of her friends, thinking she was eating seafood, discovered she had actually eaten python—a taboo in Kenyan culture. Her descriptions of the flight's takeoff and landing were so real that I dreamed about it that night. Pricilla's exceptional inspiration and motivation left a lasting impact on me, fueling my aspirations to one day experience such adventures myself.

Mr. *Maritim* was my class teacher, with approximately 15 years' teaching experience. He was well known for his teaching skills, especially in Swahili, his gifted subject. Any student taught by him lived to tell the tale. He was so good that you would be disappointed to embarrass him by scoring low in his classes. Not only was he excellent at teaching, but he was also a great storyteller when it came to passage readings. He was strict too. I remember one of my favourite friends, Ruto, accidentally playing music on his seven-melody chromo watch, a situation that got him whipped and his watch confiscated for the day to allow learning to progress. From this teacher, I learned to open up, be more friendly with the teachers, and discovered that they were humans and not animals. Consequently, I began advancing to the top three in class.

Another teacher you might like to hear about was Ibrahim, though I'm not sure if that was the correct spelling of his name or if the students had twisted it to Abraham. He was another no-nonsense scholar, tall with sleepy eyes yet always alert, and his experience was above and beyond. You could never tell if he was smiling or serious, making those of us with bad experiences in previous classes pay extra attention. He also taught math, and his inspiration was smart work: well-sectioned square books with no erasing, as that would create suspicion of a lack of confidence in your work. This was a crime punishable if you failed to prove that you knew what you were doing. He also taught us about Christian Religious Education. He was gifted, and I understand he is now retired and a servant of God, well deserved.

Fifth grade is the class where I got into a fight with a girl because she was taller and always bullied me. One day, during free period, she dared me to fight. The whole scene got the attention of the class and the neighbouring class. The fight kicked off. She was about 5 feet tall, brown, and beautiful, while I was about 4 feet and always skinny—not a perfect combo for a fight. She firmly grabbed my arms, making it hard to hit or move around. I started using wrestling tactics, kicking her in the leg several times, each kick cheered on by my classmates. The cheering gave me an added advantage; I would have gotten a million views if the fight had been captured on camera. By the tenth or eleventh kick, I saw fear in her eyes, wishing she had never started the fight in the first place. So, I decided to finish the fight by hitting her nose with my forearm, a tactic I learned from watching wrestling every Sunday. That's how I won and earned my respect back. The next day, we were friends again, but the rumour was that I was not to be joked with by any girl.

Nicknames were common back then, and if you didn't have one, it meant you weren't famous enough. I was one of the kids with a nickname based on my size; I was tiny in nearly all my classes. I remember a dare to go through a hole in one of the classrooms. Only a few of us could fit through. The trick was to get your head through first, suck in your stomach, and lastly, force your buttocks through. Everyone who succeeded was cheered on and honoured for their heroism. All these fun games happened during free lessons or when the teacher didn't show up. My classes were noisy when the teacher was not around. If you sat close to the door, you had to watch out for teachers and instruct everyone to be quiet and look busy with homework or reading. Sometimes the trick worked, but sometimes we got caught and punished for being idle and noisy. Punishments ranged from collecting rubbish in the school compound to lying down in the field and getting your buttocks whacked three to four times, depending on how noisy you were known to be.

Sixth grade was another milestone to remember, with our classroom located in the corner of an L-shaped building constructed from rough-cut lumber—the cheapest wooden material that seemed to last a lifetime. The rough lumber was uniform on the inside but uneven on the outside, with gaps that allowed us to communicate with the outside world. These holes were handy for asking friends to pass back items that had fallen outside, like a pencil, which they could simply slide through the gaps. One interesting teacher in this class was a tall fellow named Joseph, whom the classmates nicknamed "Kiplupchan" due to his habit of sweating in the mornings. These kids had a knack for coming up with fitting nicknames. Joseph was our math teacher, and his skills were exceptional, particularly in teaching angles and constructing them using a geometric set. He insisted on neat homework, and messy work could land you in trouble with him. The last thing anyone wanted at that age was to be canned by this tall and imposing figure. His presence was formidable, but his teaching left a lasting impression, making sixth grade a memorable year.

Not forgetting our seventh-grade geography and history teacher, Isaac—he was easily recognisable by his distinctive nose and unique speech. All the students paid special attention to him, especially when he taught the rich history of African leaders such as *Kwame Nkrumah*, the fascinating journey of the River Nile, the longest river in Africa, and the heroic tales of the *Mau Mau* freedom fighters. The map of Africa was practically tattooed in his brain; he could draw it flawlessly and name all the countries singlehandedly. One of his favourite tools was the compass, and woe betide the student who couldn't point out where the East was. A piece of white chalk would be thrown at you with remarkable accuracy, a testament to his precision. His chalk-throwing skills were so precise that he could have made a perfect sniper in the modern age. Despite his tough methods, Isaac's dedication and vast knowledge left a lasting impression on all of us, making geography and history unforgettable subjects.

5

If you've ever wondered how children in developing countries learn foreign languages like English, let me share my personal story with you. In pre-school, the curriculum was designed to include core subjects like English, Swahili, and Math, laying a strong educational foundation. From a young age, we were immersed in these languages, learning through songs, stories, and interactive activities that made the process enjoyable and engaging. By the end of pre-school, we were expected to read and write the letters of the alphabet, count numbers, and name colors, skills that were diligently cultivated by our dedicated teachers. English and Swahili lessons were woven into our daily routines, ensuring that we developed a solid grasp of both languages alongside our mathematical abilities. The structured yet nurturing environment fostered our cognitive development, preparing us for the more complex subjects introduced in first grade. This early education was pivotal in shaping our linguistic capabilities, enabling us to navigate a multilingual world with confidence.

In pre-school, our teacher's belief in strict discipline was evident in her frequent use of corporal punishment to enforce learning. This harsh approach, though controversial, had a certain effectiveness as it instilled a sense of urgency and motivation in us to learn quickly and accurately to avoid punishment. The classroom was meticulously divided into three rows: fast learners, average learners, and slow learners. This arrangement created a visible hierarchy that drove everyone to strive for excellence. The coveted fast learners' row was not just a mark of academic prowess but also a sanctuary from the teacher's wrath. Each day, students pushed themselves harder, eager to escape the lower rows and the looming threat of discipline. This intense atmosphere, marked by a blend of fear and determination, shaped our early educational experiences, forging a path where the desire to learn was intertwined with the drive to avoid punitive measures.

We attended school for only half a day, but the intensity of our lessons made it feel much longer, and we often envied the older kids who stayed all afternoon. Our teacher's belief that physical punishment was the quickest route to learning created a harsh and rigorous environment. It was common knowledge that if you didn't shed tears in class, you were in the wrong place. Reflecting on those days, it's clear how rough it truly was, yet there was a strange sense of equality in the shared experience. Everyone, regardless of their background, faced the same strict discipline. The simplest way to avoid the teacher's wrath was to learn quickly and score well on every test and assignment. This pressure pushed us to absorb knowledge at an impressive pace, fostering resilience and a fierce drive for academic excellence.

Most of us, including myself, preferred the tough method of discipline, though I never enjoyed it. At that young age, I hated the teacher and would cry bitterly, wanting nothing to do with him. When he was sick and missed school, we would sometimes wish he never came back. The worst part of the punishment was being pulled by the ears with a pen cap; it was excruciatingly painful. Being struck on the head with a dry stick was equally dreadful. Slapping, on the other hand, was also common and perhaps the easiest way to nip naughty behaviour in the bud. It worked every time, and I must admit, I missed watching the others being slapped, as we always cheered when it happened.

Despite the harsh methods, punishment had an undeniable impact as it pushed us to learn quickly and effectively. Our classroom was organised into three distinct rows: slow learners, average learners, and fast learners. This arrangement created a competitive atmosphere where everyone was eager to move up to the fast learners' row. The fast learners' row represented not only academic achievement but also a reprieve from the teacher's strict discipline. The desire to avoid punishment and gain recognition drove us to study harder, pay closer attention, and perform better on assignments and tests. This structured environment, though tough, instilled in us a strong work ethic and a relentless pursuit of excellence, as we all strived to reach the coveted front row.

The drive to move to the fast learners' row was intense. Counting was taught early on, and at a young age, my curiosity about learning was high. I was one of the pupils who picked up counting very quickly. We were also taught manners, such as excusing ourselves to go to the toilet. I could say a sentence in English and Swahili asking for permission to go outside, use the toilet, or sit down.

Proper etiquette was a big deal. If you entered the classroom without knocking on the door, the teacher would get upset and ask if you were entering a toilet. If this happened, a good student would go back outside, knock on the door, and say, "Teacher, may I come inside?" We were corrected every time we did not get it right and sometimes got in trouble if we kept repeating the same mistake.

Some classmates struggled significantly with constructing sentences and communicating effectively. When they wanted attention from the teacher, they would stand up silently, waiting patiently for the teacher to notice them, often enduring long moments of being overlooked. The more adept pupils would try to help, whispering phrases and sentences for them to repeat. Sometimes these efforts succeeded, and the struggling students managed to express themselves correctly. More often than not, however, their attempts were muddled and unsuccessful, leaving them frustrated and anxious. Consequently, these students often had to wait until breaks to attend to their needs or queries, when the classroom's formal structure momentarily dissolved, and they could seek help more freely from friends and peers without the pressure of performing in front of the whole class. This dynamic highlighted both the challenges they faced and the camaraderie among students as they navigated their educational journey together.

In fourth grade, the introduction of the "disk" brought a new level of motivation and dread to our classroom. These disks were worn around the neck, conspicuously made from brightly coloured plastic in shades like yellow, green, or red. Their purpose was clear: to serve as a visible mark of shame for those who fell short in their studies or behaviour. The worst of these disks were made from cowhide, exuding a constant unpleasant odour that added to their repulsiveness. Designed to be as unattractive as possible, these disks were universally despised. No one wanted to wear them, and even friends and siblings, who usually stood by each other, recoiled at the sight of the disks, avoiding those who had to wear them. The mere threat of having to don one of these odious disks was enough to spur us all into action, striving to avoid the humiliation they represented.

The purpose of the disk was to force students to speak in foreign languages and discourage the use of vernacular languages. The disk was given to anyone caught speaking their mother tongue. At the end of the day, during assembly, the disk holders had to name who gave them the disk, tracing it back to the initial holder, and everyone involved would be punished, usually with corporal punishment.

The disk system didn't last long because it was often abused. Kids destroyed the disks to avoid trouble, leading teachers to switch to a "CID" system where students secretly monitored their peers and reported anyone speaking in their mother tongue.

The CID system worked for a while, improving language skills and reducing noise in the classroom. However, it also created enmity among students, leading to its eventual downfall. Teachers began to suspect something was wrong when honest, smart students were unfairly punished. The system was eventually terminated, and responsibilities were delegated back to class monitors and prefects.

By this time, most students had naturally developed an interest in speaking English and Swahili, eager to practice and improve their language skills. This enthusiasm was reflected in a school rule mandating that upper-class students, from sixth to eighth grade, were expected to converse in English or Swahili with minimal supervision. The corridors and classrooms buzzed with the sounds of students diligently speaking these languages, turning every interaction into an opportunity for practice. Teachers found that the rule required little enforcement, as students were motivated by a genuine desire to master these languages. This shift not only enhanced their linguistic abilities but also fostered a sense of pride and confidence, preparing them for future academic and social endeavours where proficiency in English and Swahili would be invaluable. The atmosphere was one of mutual encouragement and collective growth, with students helping each other and embracing the challenge with determination and enthusiasm.

Competition with local boarding schools also played a role in our language learning. Friends who attended these schools often returned home speaking impeccable Swahili, motivating us to improve our language skills.

We focused on writing and speaking, aiming to keep up with our boarding school peers.

Language learning wasn't just about academics; it was also a social endeavour. The desire to communicate effectively with friends from boarding schools and pride in speaking a new language drove us to practice diligently. Over time, our proficiency in English and Swahili improved, benefiting both our education and social interactions.

My journey of learning English and Swahili in a developing country was marked by both challenges and triumphs. The strict discipline enforced by our teachers, coupled with innovative systems like the introduction of language rules and the motivational use of rewards and punishments, played crucial roles in our language acquisition. Social motivations, such as the desire to move up in class rankings and avoid public embarrassment, further spurred our efforts. This experience underscored the importance of perseverance and adaptation, as we navigated through various obstacles and seized every opportunity to improve. Community support, from classmates helping each other to the collective encouragement from family and teachers, was invaluable in overcoming these educational hurdles. It was a testament to how determination, combined with a supportive environment, can lead to significant achievements in even the most challenging circumstances.

6

Kabusare Primary School was one of the main elementary schools in my district before other neighboring schools were built for convenience. To get to school faster, sometimes you had to cut across someone's farm, and some paths passed right in front of people's houses, mostly their kitchens, resulting in different reactions. Generous families would greet you and talk to you about various random things, consuming your time. Sometimes they invite you inside to grab something to eat quickly. However, you wouldn't want to accept this invitation because sometimes they would tell you that the food or tea was ready, but if you took a chance to go inside, you would find out that cooking had just begun. You would then have to sit down for another fifteen to twenty minutes to wait, and sometimes the food was not worth the wait.

What was not worth the wait was tea without sugar and limited milk; we call it sugarless tea or *ntupia* in our language. The name originated from an unknown person, probably an expert in name calling. I don't know where he got it from, but based on his description, the colour was similar to muddy water, and it made perfect sense. The other food was Ugali with black nightshade or broad leafy vegetables, which could grow out of nothing and was a good habitat for snails. We heard many stories about people consuming snails without their knowledge, thinking it was meat, only to realise it was snails. The worst part of the story was some women being kicked out of their houses for a few days for being careless and feeding their spouses substandard meals.

The main means of transportation to school were your two legs and nothing else unless you were lucky to run into a generous man riding a bicycle who offered a ride without you asking. We were required to be at school at 7:30 a.m., and anyone who showed up late—meaning 7:31 a.m. onwards—got whacked by the teacher waiting impatiently at the gate. We didn't own any watches, but we were smart enough to estimate the time between home and school. I knew it took me about twenty minutes to get to school, stop time not accounted for. That meant if you stopped to pee, greet anyone, or wait for a friend, it would cost you a bit of whacking or increased speed to make up for the lost time. Our parents were very responsible and made sure we left home on time and did not show up late to school. My mother always woke up very early to milk the cows and make breakfast early.

Lunch time was 12:45 p.m., and nearly 99 percent of the students left for home to eat lunch but were required to be back in class at 2:00 p.m. The time allocated is only an hour and fifteen minutes, and sometimes you were unlucky to get that teacher who would ignore the clock and continue teaching until 1:00 p.m., leaving you with only an hour lunch break. Either way, you had to be in class by 2:00 p.m., period, with no excuses. The distance from my homestead to school was approximately 1.2 miles along a one-lane dirt road, a busy commercial route where most drivers and bikers paid little attention to anything that moved on the road. It was a common occurrence to have speeding vehicles pass so closely that you could feel the wind nearly blowing you off the path. Despite the inherent danger, it became a part of everyday life, something we no longer worried about but simply accepted as the norm. Back at home, the parents were busy toiling in the farm and had just returned by the time you got home, requesting your assistance in making a fire so that cooking could start, and you could make it back to school on time. The faster you got down on your knees, the faster you saw cooking action starting; if you took your time, it was vice versa. All the tasks were verbal orders, and at no given time would you dare say no because it would not go very well for you. So, with no time wasted, it was nice to help in any way possible, like fetching water, getting firewood, cooking, fetching or cutting vegetables, or even being around your parents talking as you waited.

Our kitchen was situated right along the path most kids used to pass through on their way to school, allowing us to easily identify who was heading back each day. We saw the same kids daily, leaving in the same sequence, making it easy to notice who missed school by checking with their siblings. We enjoyed eating outside under an avocado tree by the kitchen, where it was cool and smoke-free. However, this spot meant we constantly had to respond to people passing by, inviting them to stop for lunch even when we knew there wasn't enough food. This old-school practice was intended to promote generosity and sharing with those in need, but it often got misused. Even young kids would extend lunch or tea invitations, regardless of whether anyone was home. We knew certain people who would fall victim to this, actually stopping by and hanging around for hours until the mother of the house returned from the farm or firewood fetching, only to then figure out a plan for food or tea.

School kids were encouraged to be in a rush because of the saying about the earliest bird to catch the worm, and we were often told to hurry up and run to school before blessings were taken by kids from other families. Believing this, we would always rush back to school. Afternoons were always hot and sleepy, especially during geography classes taught by certain teachers who would throw a piece of chalk at anyone caught sleeping. Most lessons concluded at 3:45 p.m., after which the remaining time was used for cleaning and announcements for the next day or the rest of the week. This routine was followed every week from the beginning of the term until the end, and it was easy to stay out of trouble if you were hardworking and among the top ten in class. However, getting into trouble was just as easy, whether by taking a classmate's pen or rubber without asking or getting into a street fight and being identified.

Closing ceremonies at the end of the term were amazing. They were prepared in advance by administering end-of-term exams to all pupils. The exam took a week to complete, followed by a week of marking and grading, and then closing day when grading was completed, and students were ranked. The week after the final exam was laid back; there was not much reading to do except to sit in groups both inside and outside the class, mainly to talk about imaginary stories and play. Some kids were well known for telling funny stories, mostly portraying characters from their parents. Joel was one of them. We pronounced his name as Joeeel because it sounded better, and I think he liked it that way. *Joeeel* was and still is a gifted speaker, and so was his late father. He would make up a story and had the ability to narrate it so well that you wouldn't blink until he was done talking. I remember him narrating one of the novels by *John Kiriamiti* while we were in seventh grade. The book is about two hundred pages long, and I am sure he must have read the book over and over because he was able to narrate the whole scene without skipping anything. We loved it, enjoyed it, and above all, liked the guy so much that we would go around looking for him to tell us the plan for the day. On the other hand, his brother *Leh* was a good bully. We still liked him because he was the kind who would shape people's characters by putting them on the spot about how they dressed, talked, laughed, or even walked. His character was so unique that despite him being a bully, it was hard for him to get into trouble because he knew how to play along and get away with it.

Gambling was also common during free time as we waited for grades and the closing ceremony. Everyone was specialised in one way or another. Another character was *Kunga*; his real name was Robert, but no one knew him by his real name. The easiest way to spot him in a large group was by his two front teeth; they were huge, white, and made him appear as if he was smiling even if he was in deep trouble. His character was good. I never saw him put up a fight with anyone except when provoked. He was a ringleader in gambling. He was well known and always carried a lot of coins in his pocket, and you would think he was the son of a local politician, but he was not. I knew him because his brother *Amos* was my friend, and I got a piece of his share through his brother, who bought me candies, beef cubes, biscuits, or sometimes a quarter of bread, which regular students could not afford.

Another important group I cannot forget to mention are street fight organisers. Despite being punishable by the school authorities, fighting was a common occurrence among students, happening inside classrooms, outside on school grounds, and even on the roads. The characters involved varied from organisers and fighters to cheering squads. The organisers played a pivotal role in setting up these confrontations, often ensuring a crowd was present to witness the brawls. I made it a point to steer clear of these activities, fearing the repercussions both at school and at home. The cruelest fights often erupted during closing ceremonies, serving as a brutal send-off for opponents to mull over during the holidays. These fights could be vicious, sometimes resulting in severe injuries like near-missed eyes and frequent nosebleeds. The one silver lining was the unspoken rule that weapons were not allowed unless explicitly approved by the organisers, which, to some extent, prevented even more serious harm. The organised chaos of these fights reflected a darker side of school culture, where grudges and rivalries were settled in a violent rite of passage.

Most of the memorable memories during closing day were sitting the entire school out in the sun and a small ceremony was held. Sitting arrangement was usually boys sitting on the left side of the field while girls sat on the other side. There was always a huge gap left between the two genders. Sometimes, we were forced by the teacher on duty to connect the gap and, but it was acceptable most of the time and everyone was fine with it. Opening prayer was offered and from there class teachers beginning in first grade would stand up and present the names of students who performed the best in their final exams. Top three students were given prices which usually comprise of school supplies which increased with quality towards the higher grades. Every teacher was required to comment on performance and a word of encouragement to students who did their best and those that did not. Also, this teacher would use the chance to challenge the parents to put more effort or keep up what they are doing at home to ensure learning continues at home beside tasking their children with tasks to complete while at home.

Most of the school holidays were a month long except for December which was longer. We were encouraged to keep studying for the next term and to revise what we missed during the end of term exams, something I never did. I always tried for the first week and by the second and third week I could not pick a book to read due to my work schedule at home and catching up with friends here and there. It was a normal thing to do. We were also encouraged to stay home and help our parents with daily chores that never end. While at home, we never get time to just sit and relax, instead we constantly do tasks that range from farm work to fetching water and sometimes firewood. We liked it and we enjoyed doing it because that is what everyone else does at home. We enjoyed mealtimes because there was never a rush for school except to leave the house for the farm. Plucking tea was my favourite; my father had about five acres of tea plantations which depended on our labor. There were no casual labourers because it was expensive to maintain them and most of the work was managed by our parents. Together with my other siblings, we worked on the farm until you could not distinguish us from the labourers. We never complained, instead, we liked it and enjoyed it because it paid off.

My father was the main manager responsible for assigning us tasks each morning, and sometimes the evening before, depending on what was needed on the farm. Occasionally, our numbers would dwindle when neighbours borrowed one of us to help out, especially during harvest seasons. It was common for families to lend a hand to each other with harvesting corn, potatoes, beans, and other crops. Most of the corn harvesting took place in August, perfectly timed with the school holidays, providing an ample source of labor. We grew up with this routine, and it was a normal part of life. Missing out on a ride in a tractor while on the farm meant missing out on a lot of fun. A few wealthy individuals owned tractors back then, most of which were old, poorly maintained, and often needed to be pushed to start due to the absence of key starters. Kids were usually enlisted to push the tractors and were rewarded with rides in return. Families with large corn farms would rent tractors for transportation, which was a major attraction for all the boys in the village. Whenever they heard the sound of a tractor during harvest time, they would flock to the fields without needing an invitation, except for those from strict families who weren't allowed to participate in such events.

Our elder brother was responsible for our safety because he was more advanced in how to get on and off the tractor. It was easy to lose teeth because the drivers never cared about safety or running over anyone. Their job was just to pay attention to where they were driving and if their locally made cigarette was burning. Normally you would smoke a few feet from a tractor, but these guys would use the exhaust of a tractor to ignite a cigarette. That's how careless they were. Also, they were good at cursing and calling kids names and sometimes they would whip you if they didn't like how you looked. You were not lucky if you were missing front milk teeth. It is funny that nearly all the boys who showed up for tractor rides had either missing teeth, funny haircuts or thorny clothes. Such characters also made perfect candidates for fighting because other bullies would use the chance to make fun of them and sometimes, they would not take the joke lightly.

I got away with all sorts of mishaps except one night when we were chasing down a tractor to jump on for an illegal ride. It did not go very well. My older brother was the first one to jump on, of course because he was older and was able to run faster than most of us and I was the second one. I was able to hang onto a tractor for a couple of minutes but when it was time to jump off, I overheard my brother talking about jumping and hanging onto the tractor as you run and let it go. It did not make sense at all. So, I decided to jump off without following his protocols and as soon as I landed on the road, I fell down and saw sparkling-we used to call stars when you get a concussion. Instead of asking if I was OK, the other guys laughed at me while I screamed and yelled my mother's name because it was funny and stupid at the same time. When laughed off, usually the victim would turn wild and hit whoever was laughing at him but this time round I was not able to hit anyone because it was dark and I thought I had lost some of my teeth but luckily, I did not. From that day, I learnt my lesson and I never ran after a moving tractor anyhow and if I did, I always approached it with caution.

Tea farming is one of the most tedious jobs, but when you grow up with it, it becomes routine and part of your lifestyle, making it seem normal. Every morning, we'd wake up, have a cup of tea, grab a basket, and head down to the farm to pick tea for hours. After that, we would transport the tea to a buying centre. Since tea is perishable, it needs to be trans-ported to a processing factory within a few hours, but this rarely happens. Instead, the tea would often sit in the buying centre for days, sometimes up to three days. Three days was the worst, as the tea would go bad and sometimes be rejected by the clerk. The tea was weighed in 12-kilogram bags, commonly called sacks, and you could only weigh your tea if you had these bags. Obtaining the bags was a challenge and sometimes a matter of life and death; we knew of people who had been run over by the company lorry in their attempts to get them. The sacks were distributed on a first-come, first-served basis. If you choose to sit and wait, you might never get to sell your tea, resulting in no earnings and wasted effort for the family. We struggled, often staying at the buying centre overnight, waiting for the company lorry to arrive. Sometimes it came late at night, and sometimes early in the morning after we had just left. Together with my brother and father, we switched shifts for meals and showers, making sure someone was always there to secure our place and ensure we could sell our tea.

I was good at securing sacks and rarely missed out on getting one. When I did miss, I had several friends to borrow from, though sometimes we had to wait for the next shift, which could be eight hours later or even the next day. We called it the holiday routine because the produce was high due to all the students being home in the village. It was often frustrating, and we wished for better things to do besides pick tea and wait to sell it to the local tea processing factory. However, the pay was very good. At the end of the month, our parents received substantial payments, and everyone was happy, momentarily forgetting the hard labor and the tedious process. We benefited as well, enjoying steak dinners, incentives, and sometimes shopping, though most of the money went towards education. Meanwhile, kids whose parents were teachers or government workers had nothing to do with these chores. They stayed home, watching TV, hanging out, or drinking tea with their legs crossed. We admired their life-style, but our parents constantly reminded us that their parents had worked hard, and we needed to work hard for ourselves.

7

Some of the most memorable moments in primary school were during sports seasons, school trips, and academic trophy ceremonies. Our school year was divided into three terms, akin to seasons in Western education. The first term was the athletic season, a time I particularly enjoyed even though I didn't participate in any running events. I revealed in watching the senior students practice and compete. Their dedication and skill inspire us all. The second term was dedicated to soccer, a sport that brought the entire school together in shared enthusiasm, with lively matches and spirited cheering. The school pioneers and sportsmen included my cousin Kipkirui Bor, known for his tall stature, long legs, and high thinking capacity. Another notable pioneer was Mario, celebrated for his creativity and public speaking skills. Then there were Jonah, Kosiko, and Charles, whom we nicknamed "the driver." I got to know these individuals during a 4x400 meter relay. Their running skills and speed were so remarkable that they could have earned gold medals in the modern era. Their performance was impressive and exceptional, and if captured on video, it would have made an excellent scene in a movie.

The third term focused on drama and music festivals, vibrant events showcasing the creative talents of our peers. Unfortunately, participation in these festivals was usually reserved for the upper classes, leaving us in the lower grades to admire from the sidelines. Despite this, the excitement and cultural richness of these festivals were contagious, filling the school with energy and anticipation. Each of these terms brought its own unique experiences and highlights, making the school year a dynamic and memorable journey.

A circular letter from the zone was sent to our game teacher with the sports day schedule. An assembly was then called, usually before lunch, to pass the message on to all pupils. Most of the athletic events were scheduled at least a month in advance to give the competitors time to practice and get ready for the competition. I liked watching practice sessions. We would sit for hours after classes just to watch the upper classes practice and compete against each other. Sometimes, they would pass out at the end of the run, which the games teacher explained was due to a lack of oxygen. We enjoyed watching them as they passed out and seeing how first aid was administered by an expert at that time. The most common first aid I witnessed was blowing air on the victim's face using a sweater until they returned to consciousness. We never got to witness other serious injuries that required immediate medical attention, but if that happened, parents were involved before taking the athlete to the hospital.

As kids, we were really good at tracking the calendar for these events so we could prepare in advance by saving money for lunches and snacks. Among the four primary schools in the zone, our school was always the host because we had a bigger playground and better resources compared to the other schools. Competitions were usually scheduled for Fridays because they took the whole day and left the school compound very dirty from food remains like corn cobs, sugarcane peels, mango peels, and plastic wraps from all assorted candies. All pupils were encouraged to let their parents know about the upcoming events so they could prepare food for sale during that day. Common foods for sale include mashed potatoes, porridge, *githeri* (mixed corn and beans), chapatti, *mandazi*, *mahamri*, and rice, among others. There was also a variety of fruits such as mangoes, oranges, passion fruits, avocados, loquats, sliced pineapples, and sugar canes. Other commercial foods include candies, cookies, sodas, and frozen popsicle.

Most of us were encouraged to take food with us to school during sports days, but we preferred to buy it because it was an awesome thing to do and a perfect time to use all our savings. Most of the savings came from selling eggs and hens, while some kids from richer families were given money. I was very good at budgeting for money and sometimes had some left at the end of the day. Coins were common, and it was easy to tell who had more money just by the noise when running around and the weight of their pockets. I don't remember the last time I carried coins in my pocket because it's annoying, but back then, you weren't a real boy if you didn't have coins in your pocket. Losing them was a bad day for you, especially if you had planned what to buy with them. You were mistaken for a conman if you ordered something only to realise that the money was missing. On the other hand, for the one who found the money, it was a gain because it meant more money to spend.

Stealing was a common but discouraged behaviour in our

school, with certain individuals notorious for threatening to take others' food or money by force. Among these, one boy stood out—a skinny, short figure with a perpetually sweating nose, a trait that, according to local rumour, signalled a thief's lineage. Whether or not this was true, his actions suggested he might have been influenced by his home environment. Despite his small stature, he was fierce and unyielding, always ready to fight and never accepting defeat. If he lost a fight, he would relentlessly challenge his opponent again, even resorting to bringing a weapon if necessary. His intimidating presence cast a shadow over our fun, making us wary and cautious. Yet, we learned to navigate around his threats. The most effective tactic was enlisting the help of an older sibling or neighbour to confront and rebuke him. A stern warning from a respected elder was often enough to keep him at bay, ensuring he wouldn't return to trouble us again. This boy, with his relentless aggression, was a unique challenge in our school life, but one we managed to overcome with the support of our community.

Despite the various challenges that could have hindered our enjoyment during sports time, we always managed to have fun and forget about everything else. Having friends was invaluable, as they were always there during crises, sharing whatever they had, including buying you food when you had none. My mother had a sugar cane plantation, and I would often take a piece to school to share with a friend who didn't have any, in return for something else. With up to three friends, I had access to three different food options. Another fun activity was walking around the temporary marketplace looking for lost coins. Occasionally, we would run into an adult who knew us and would buy us something. These moments of camaraderie and small adventures made our days enjoyable and memorable.

The competition always began with all participating schools gathering to have their games teachers introduce themselves and their roles. It was refreshing to hear from new teachers, as we were accustomed to our own, and we enjoyed listening to different voices. These teachers often teased about their teams' strength and their certainty of winning, making us nervous even if we weren't participants. The main emphasis was safety and enthusiastic cheering. After the speeches and the announcement of the day's lineup, each school was assigned a sitting spot, usually the same one each time. The differences between schools were easily distinguishable by their uniforms and the number of students. Our host school always had the largest contingent, followed by the second largest school, which brought many civilian cheer squads. Interestingly, most of these cheerers were short and always carried rungus, the wooden Maasai clubs typically used when herding cows.

Competitions went on for hours, with kids all over the field screaming instead of cheering. To the older folks, it was annoying, but for us, it was the perfect event we had eagerly waited for a long time. I would scream at the top of my lungs, and the next day my throat would be sore, and my voice lost. A big chalkboard was brought outside to keep track of the scores, which were updated and announced at intervals to keep the teams fired up and motivated. By noon, it was easy to tell which team was winning or losing just by looking at the score gap, the remaining events, and the probability of each team's success. Our school was often at the top, followed by the other large schools. After the local competitions, all the teams would unite to form one team to compete at the Zonal level. The Zonal competition featured more schools, intense competition, and a lot of cheering. Being young, I was restricted from attending because it was far away, and my parents were concerned about the risks of getting lost or bullied by strangers at the event.

Even though we missed the zonal competition, my older siblings would brief us every time they got back from sports, and it was just the same as attending. We liked to hear how some of our famous athletes performed, and it was saddening to hear some of them getting defeated and not being able to proceed to the district level. After the zonal competition, the competition became more intense and further away. I remember my older brother and cousin were still able to attend. It was a distance of about 20 miles, and they would leave in the morning and be back in the evening.

Time changed, and when I was in seventh and eighth grade, I was able to attend such events. Soccer was my favourite. We had this guy named *Terer* but who went by the nickname "Q", who was really good. He played to impress, and sometimes you would think you were watching it on television. Soccer was a big sport, and most people liked it. Whether old or young, they all came to watch, cheer, drink porridge, and eat roasted corn. One of the games teachers liked drinking, and I remember him spilling the beans during one of the matches in a county stadium. I don't know what he drank, but he was so drunk that he could barely walk, talk, or turn around. Every time he tried to cheer on his favourite player, he would fall down over and over and keep rolling in front of thousands of pupils. When that happened, he became the centre of interest. He was so drunk that we began to like him a lot because of his unstable gait and the general appearance of his eyes and mouth.

On the other hand, there was another teacher named *Ndinga*, though I understand it was a nickname he preferred. He carried a whistle like a necklace and a *rungu* on his waist, always visible in his double-vented suit. To a visitor unfamiliar with him, he might appear to be a local farmer. *Ndinga's* main job was to lead the cheering squad, which included both opponents and the team. He was liked by many, and any kid could join in cheering with him regardless of their team allegiance. The main reason for his popularity was his dance moves. At the end of every game, he would blow his whistle and lead the cheerers in a unique dance that was unforgettable. As a kid, you couldn't afford to miss *Ndinga's* dance. It was good, memorable, and always perfectly timed to end the event on a high note.

Mr. Jackson Towett was another English scholar you wouldn't want to miss hearing about. I knew him even before he began his teaching career, thanks to the *Kipchamba* music he played in the evenings, audible from the other side of the village. Tall and possessing intelligent eyes, he had the best handwriting one could imagine. The first time I saw him teaching, he wore a bright red woven sweater and a shirt in true British style—clean, hand-washed, and dried according to the manufacturer's instructions. His shoes were always polished to a shine, and his hair was meticulously combed. His attention to detail in grooming made it nearly impossible to find areas for improvement. Mr. Towett's English, both spoken and written, was fluent and rich with vocabulary, often making it hard for some of us to keep up. To this day, he still offers me new vocabulary to use while traveling. His English intelligence and impeccable dress code conveyed a clear message: he was there to install knowledge and excellence.

8

I spent two years in seventh and eighth grade, a common practice back in the days for various reasons. While some students were retained due to poor performance, needing an additional year to catch up and be prepared for the next grade, my situation was different. I excelled academically, but my parents faced the challenge of managing tuition fees for my older siblings who were in higher classes. To ensure that none of us had to drop out of school, they decided to evenly distribute our education timelines. I embraced this arrangement without any resentment, viewing it as an opportunity rather than a setback. The extra years allowed me to delve deeper into my studies, solidifying my knowledge and skills. It was a time of personal growth and academic enrichment, and I appreciated the chance to prepare myself thoroughly for the future while supporting my family's needs.

By this grade, I was fully mature and knew what was going on around the world just by reading old newspapers and listening to the radio. Here is also where I met other teachers who had 20 years' experience if not more. Mr. Rotich was the epitome of professionalism and precision. His smart grey hair was always neatly trimmed, adding a distinguished air to his appearance. He dressed impeccably, in crisp shirts and polished shoes, embodying cleanliness and order. Known for his strict demeanour, he commanded respect effortlessly; his mere presence in the classroom ensured that students maintained their best behaviour. What set Mr. Rotich apart were his excellent vision and hearing skills; nothing escaped his notice. He could spot a scribbled note being passed or hear a whispered comment from across the room. His perceptive nature made him an incredibly effective teacher, able to address issues before they escalated and always staying one step ahead of his students. His high standards and keen senses created an environment where excellence was the norm, and his students knew they had to rise to meet his expectations.

Francis loved sports and, on that day, he decided, oh well, let me take these eight graders for physical exercise. That specific day, the sun blazed brightly in the clear blue sky, casting a golden glow over everything it touched. The air was warm, but a steady, playful wind danced through the scene, rustling leaves and making tree branches sway gently. The wind carried the scent of blooming flowers and freshly cut grass, adding a refreshing note to a sunny day. The wind and sun together created a perfect balance, making it a day that was both vibrant and invigorating, full of the energy and promise that only such weather can bring. It was perfect for a run. He led us in a warmup exercise and divided us into groups of four to five individuals to race against each other in a 200M race.

The first group took off, then the second, third and so forth as we cheered each other on. It was fun and it didn't take long before we were sent back to a class for the next lesson which was music taught by *Mr. Sigei* also known as *Mbou*. Mr. *Sigei* towered over the students, his height making him an imposing figure in the classroom. He always wore rubber shoes that squeaked softly with each step, adding to his unique presence. His beard was full and unruly, a dark mass that covered most of his face and seemed to have a life of its own. Complementing his wild beard was his uncombed hair, which stuck out in every direction as if in perpetual rebellion against any attempt at taming. Despite his rugged appearance, his eyes held sharp intelligence, and he had a way of commanding attention without saying a word. The students were always attentive, partly out of respect and partly out of curiosity, wondering what this intriguing figure would say or do next.

The classroom was a whirlwind of chaos as students, exhausted from a grueling 200-meter race, staggered in, collapsing onto their desks or the floor, gasping for breath. Some fanned themselves with notebooks, while others sprawled out dramatically, limbs akimbo, as if they had just finished a marathon. Amidst the pandemonium, their teacher, Mr. Sigei, stood at the front with a mischievous grin. He chuckled, shaking his head, and said, "You'd think we ran a 200-mile race instead of 200 meters!" His lighthearted teasing added to the mix of laughter and groans echoing through the room. The atmosphere was a blend of fatigue and amusement, with students both laughing at themselves and relishing the brief respite from their usual studies. It didn't last long when everyone got back to normal, and the music lesson started.

Mr. Sigei's music lesson was the highlight of the week for the students.

As soon as he entered the room, his infectious cheerfulness filled the air. He started with a joke that had everyone laughing before it even began. With a broad smile, he picked up his imaginary guitar and strummed a lively tune, encouraging everyone to join in. His voice, rich and melodious, led the students through a series of songs, each one more upbeat than the last. Mr. Sigei didn't just teach; he performed, dancing around the room with exaggerated, funny moves that had everyone giggling. He made sure each student felt included, often pulling them up to dance alongside him or leading a call-and-response song that echoed joyfully through the classroom. By the end of the lesson, the room was buzzing with energy, every student singing, clapping, and moving to the rhythm, their spirits lifted by Mr. Sigei's boundless enthusiasm and love for music.

Mr. Sigei, known for his usually cheerful demeanour, took on a stern and serious air as he addressed the class. The students, who had failed to score at least 60% on their recent test, lined up nervously. In his hand, he held a "Ngatumiat," a thin, flexible stick traditionally used for discipline. His expression was a mix of disappointment and determination as he prepared to enforce the school's strict standards. Each student winced in anticipation; the classroom's usual lighthearted atmosphere was replaced with tension. As he administered the punishment, his strokes were swift and precise, a reminder of the high expectations he held for his pupils. Despite the harsh discipline, there was an underlying message of wanting them to strive for better, to push beyond their limits, and to understand the importance of hard work and dedication. For those of us who achieved the required score,

Mr. Sigei's reminder that we needed to do better next time was a wake-up call. His expectations were higher for some of us, and he was right—we shouldn't be content with just scoring average but should always aim higher. His expectations not only set a standard but also served as a constant reminder that we had the potential to excel.

9

It didn't take long before I sat for the Kenya Certificate of Primary Education (K.C.P.E), the crucial exam required for entry into high school. This comprehensive exam was graded out of 700 marks, covering seven subjects: English, Swahili, Math, Science and Agriculture, Geography, History and Religious Education (GHCRE), and Art, Craft, and Music. Administered in October, the anticipation for the results stretched over the next few months, with the outcome typically announced after Christmas. Those three months were filled with a mixture of anxiety and hope, as we all awaited the results that would determine our academic futures. The K.C.P.E. was more than just a test; it was a rite of passage, marking the transition from primary to secondary education, and the effort and dedication invested in preparing for it was monumental.

As the K.C.S.E exam approached, the atmosphere at the school grew increasingly intense. Students, aware of the high stakes, dedicated every spare moment to studying. The classrooms and libraries were filled with the soft rustle of pages turning and the faint murmur of whispered revisions.

Late into the night, the glow of lanterns and the flicker of flashlights could be seen in the homes where students poured over their notes, eyes strained but determined.

In the weeks leading up to the exams, the school organised special prayer sessions. Students, teachers, and even some parents gathered in the assembly hall, their voices united in earnest supplication. The air was thick with the scent of incense and the weight of collective hopes and fears. Kneeling together, they prayed fervently, seeking divine intervention for strength, clarity, and success. The prayers were intense and heartfelt, each student silently promising to do their best, driven by the desire not to disappoint their parents and teachers.

The fear of failure loomed large, not just as a personal setback, but as a potential embarrassment for their entire village. The pressure was palpable; these exams were more than just a measure of academic ability—they were a rite of passage, a chance to honour their community and secure a brighter future. The weight of expectation hung heavily on their young shoulders, but amidst the anxiety, there was also a sense of solidarity and shared purpose.

As the day of the exams finally dawned, the students, buoyed by their preparation and prayers, walked into the examination hall with a mix of nerves and quiet resolve. They knew that their hard work and the hopes of their families and teachers rode on their performance, and they were determined to make everyone proud.

After three months, the official results were announced over the radio, recognising the top-performing schools and candidates. During this time, every student who had taken the exam was filled with anxiety, fearing poor performance and the prospect of being retained in the same class, unable to join their desired high school. Academic affairs lacked privacy, and much of the anxiety stemmed from the fact that the results were displayed in a glass window for everyone to see, leaving no room to lie about your scores. This public display made poor performance one of the worst days for many students, while it was an exciting moment for the top scorers. Poor performance brought shame not only to oneself but also to one's family and school. Fortunately, I did very well, scoring 460 out of 700 on my second attempt, which was good enough to join the high school of my choice. I was offered admission letter to Kabungut High School, one of the provincial high schools in the Rift Valley that admits bright students. I was both excited and overwhelmed by the fear of what lay ahead. My parents were thrilled for me, and I was confident I would join the school. However, things did not go as planned, and instead, I was asked to join one of the local day schools established by the same primary school I had attended for nine years.

As the sun set, casting a warm glow over their modest home, my father sat with me at the wooden kitchen table, his voice gentle yet earnest. "I know you've dreamed of attending that prestigious high school in the city," he began, his eyes reflecting both love and concern. "But our financial situation makes it difficult." He paused, reaching out to hold my hand. "Attending the local high school will not only ease our burden, but it will also allow you to stay close to your family, to be here for your younger siblings." His voice softened, filled with conviction. "I promise you, education is not just about the place, but about the effort you put in. If you stay here, I can bless you with the little I have, and together we can ensure you still reach your dreams." I listened intently, feeling the depth of his father's love and the sacrifices he was willing to make. My father's heartfelt words, coupled with his unwavering support, painted a future where staying local was not a compromise, but a different path to the same success.

The choice of which high school to attend was critically important, as it was often seen as a predictor of future academic success and the likelihood of university admission. Students who performed well in their K.C.P.E were admitted to prestigious national or provincial high schools, which were renowned for their excellent performance, high scores, and almost guaranteed pathways to public universities after four years. Being accepted into these schools was a source of immense pride and a promising future. On the other hand, students who ended up in local day schools faced significant disadvantages. These schools often lacked the resources and infrastructure to provide the same quality of education, despite following the same syllabus. I always felt the system was discriminatory, as it perpetuated inequality based on the school's resources rather than the student's potential. This disparity highlighted a fundamental flaw in the education system, where access to quality education was unevenly distributed, creating barriers for many talented students in less privileged schools.

After sitting down with my dad for hours as he explained his decision, I accepted it and took my results to the local day school to ask for admission. I was easily admitted due to my high qualifications, becoming admission number eighty-six, meaning only 85 students had been admitted before me. Life was rough because the same classroom where I had started first grade was now turned into ninth grade, which was hard to believe. I accepted that it was high school and separate from primary school, but the most disappointing aspect was seeing the same primary school teachers who had expected me to be elsewhere. Their eyes seemed full of disbelief, but my attitude was different. Since joining high school, I felt different, and my knowledge began to increase. I was maturing every day and becoming smarter.

The school later became a part-day and part-boarding school, with boarding being optional based on applications and bed availability in the dormitory. I applied and was approved, even though my home was only a few miles away. I did not want to keep walking back and forth, as I saw it as a waste of time and wanted to experience something different in high school. I wanted to experience boarding school. While most of my friends preferred going back home for better meals and weekends, I gave up all that to focus on studying. Not many would find it easy, but it was easy for me because I knew what I was after. There were bullies, too; some seniors and transfers would bully us and call us names. The common name was "mono" or "form one" for ninth graders. I never knew some people could be so mean and willing to spend their entire high school career bullying others. Ironically, these same people would also complain about the quality of food served in the kitchen.

Boarding life in secondary school was fun, despite the lack of tap water. We relied on a well, which often ran dry due to high demand, forcing us to travel kilometres to fetch water from a stream. The journey was tough, as the terrain to the river source was rough and steep, making carrying a five-litre container of water feel like climbing Mt. Kilimanjaro. As we ascended the hill, we had to sip the water, and by the time we reached our destination, friends were already lined up with cups, begging for a sip of the fresh water. This rationing left us with about 2.5 litres to wash our heads and get ready for class the next day.

The facility lacked electricity, so we relied on pressure lamps, which worked well but sometimes failed due to wear and tear. Prep time, dedicated to studying and homework after dinner, was illuminated by these lamps. Dinner was served in a military style, with the bell ringing to signal mealtime. Some students, already hovering around the kitchen and salivating at the aroma, begged for a sample—a behaviour not tolerated by the cooks. This was also the time when clever students would distract the cook so others could sneak some extra soup to share later. The food was satisfying, but there was a special diet group that claimed medical conditions to avoid certain foods and receive the limited commodity of milk. Most were likely fabricating their conditions to get special treatment. The limited milk supply forced some students to sneak home and bring their own.

During prep time in our co-ed school, the seating arrangements were often modified to suit the needs of certain boys. It was common to see couples pretending to discuss schoolwork, but their appearance revealed otherwise—one was clearly being seduced, evident from their looks and sweaty faces. These couples would often beg to have the prep hours extended for their benefit. At around 10 PM, the lights were turned off, and everyone returned to their dormitories. The dormitory was packed with bunk beds, offering no privacy, with each twin bed shared by two occupants. Being small, I was an ideal bunkmate, as it allowed the other person more space. Despite the rats scrambling for leftover food in the nearby storage room, the quality of sleep was surprisingly top-notch. Boarding in a dormitory was also filled with horror stories from neighbouring schools about night runners performing rituals on students during the night, but fortunately, my group never encountered such situations.

I recall a few instances when a group of students organised a protest that I found to be misguided and impractical. One memorable occasion involved the timekeeper, who was responsible for ringing the bell according to the day's schedule, being instructed not to ring it for lunch. Instead, we were herded outside for an unscheduled meeting orchestrated by a group of dissatisfied students. The agenda wasn't about academics or the quality of our education; it revolved around the monotonous nature of our lunch menu. Githeri, a hearty mix of beans and corn, was our staple meal. It was cheap, nutritious, and easy to prepare in large quantities, always served hot and enriched with fats, salt, and all the essentials for a satisfying lunch. However, these students demanded more luxurious meals—meat, rice, fruits—that were far beyond the school's budget. I couldn't help but think about how unrealistic and shortsighted their demands were, imagining them foolishly trying to manage the school's finances. Their inability to appreciate the practicality of our meals and their disregard for the larger community's well-being highlighted their immaturity and lack of foresight, leaving me exasperated by their actions.

Sometimes their grievances were valid, but I always thought there were better ways to handle them than just disrupting learning in the entire school. Most of this was influenced by neighbouring high schools and transfers from bigger schools with better meal plans. Still, it was stupid because they were already here at the local school seeking a better life like every other student. Most of us came from the same family backgrounds and knew how home was like, and none of this would be unknown at home. The ringleaders always made sure it was kept within the school. The word on the street would sometimes get them in trouble back home for leading such strikes. So, if you thought they were brave, no, they were cowards of the highest order. They could still be whipped even by their mothers at home.

Leadership was also discovered in me while in high school. It was both challenging and fun. I learned to get along with my comrades and lead by example. Leadership shaped me into a better person because I always put the needs of others ahead of mine. I also used the privilege to connect with teachers because as leaders, we were expected to go to the staffroom to replace filled books or ask general questions and raise concerns. The more I connected with teachers, the better I learned about their characters and how I could fit in and ask for encouragement from those I trusted the most. There were ups and downs in leadership. I used the position to my advantage to get the resources I needed to succeed and be closer to those above me for support. On the other hand, there was too much expectation from the school and those I was leading. Together with other class leaders, we were always expected to do our best and set a good example for the rest of the school. We might have been taken advantage of by those above us because we were trusted, but we always made sure to use them to our advantage.

I enjoyed school a lot. We had sports, and teachers were switching back and forth because most were privately paid for by parents. We were lucky to have a headteacher and his deputy finally sent by the Teachers' Service Commission. Principal Mr. M.K. Cheruiyot was a towering figure, both in stature and presence. A veteran of the National Youth Service (NYS), he carried himself with the disciplined air of someone who had seen and done it all. Tall and handsome, with a chiseled jawline and a confident stride, he was a man who turned heads wherever he went. His sharp suits, always impeccably tailored, and polished shoes made him the epitome of elegance and authority.

During M. K.'s time, I was appointed as the school captain, a highly respected position typically offered to a student with good character and a strong academic background. While this role was equivalent to that of a president in more developed secondary schools, my experience was different and filled with challenges. I had to supervise my peers in performing simple tasks and was sometimes misused by the staff for unrelated tasks, such as running errands. However, I used the position to my advantage, as I was entrusted with keys to essential authority spaces, which I and other serious scholars used for class discussions and private studies. The role also allowed me to request additional writing materials and resources off the record, requests that were never denied. The position paid off during sports trips, where I could board the bus as a non-player without question. This forced the games teacher to adjust the budget to ensure I was fed with bread and soda for lunch, a luxurious meal compared to the packed cold food other schools had to bring from their kitchens. Our commercially bought lunch set us apart and put us at the top. The role of school captain also came with a name tag bearing the word "Captain" on the right chest, granting me the privilege of entering any office within the school compound, sometimes even without knocking. A teammate who held the same position on the girl's side was Philomena, a name of Greek origin. She was tall, with beautiful eyes, a well-balanced nose in relation to the rest of her face, a smaller tip, symmetrical nostrils, and a smooth profile. Her beauty was extraordinary, likely inherited from her mother. A Catholic, Philomena had a unique singing voice and remarkable confidence. Her leadership style was phenomenal, making her a role model admired by everyone.

Mr. Cheruiyot was a no-nonsense educator, known for his strict adherence to discipline and high standards. Under his leadership, the high school underwent a remarkable transformation. He instilled a culture of excellence, demanding the best from both students and teachers. Lateness, sloppiness, and mediocrity had no place in his school. His keen eye for detail and unwavering commitment to quality education quickly turned the school into a model of success.

But it wasn't just his strictness that earned him respect; it was also his undeniable charisma and genuine care for his students' futures. He frequently walked the halls, his keen eyes missing nothing, yet he was always ready with a word of encouragement or a piece of advice. His presence was both inspiring and intimidating, a blend that motivated everyone to rise to the occasion. Under his transformative leadership, academic performance soared, school facilities improved, and a sense of pride and purpose permeated the campus. Mr. Cheruiyot was not just a principal; he was a beacon of excellence.

During M. K's leadership, he organised and approved the identification processing at school. My connection with this remarkable man was top-notch. When I brought the request to him, he did not question it and, through his connections, brought the entire registration department to the school—something that had never been done before. While a few skeptics viewed it negatively, for many of us, it was a crucial step toward bigger things in life. Obtaining a legal identification card after high school was a significant milestone, enabling us to move forward with greater opportunities.

Another memorable moment created by M.K was the introduction of weekend entertainment. The school did not own a television, and that's when Charles Towett, a well-known electrician, stepped in to save the day. Whether it was his career or just a gift, his talent for electronics was magical. Not only did he provide entertainment for the entire weekend, but he could also build a radio from scratch. Charles, a short, clean, and well-shaved individual, was always sportily dressed and kept up with the latest shoes on the market. He was also the proud owner of a 7-speed bicycle. His presentations on entertainment days left the whole school begging for more Nigerian movies. His descriptions and snapshots of movies like Rambo left us with our mouths open, and his skills with a complex remote were admirable. We loved him, and he dedicated his entire weekend to entertaining the whole school with movies. Being handed the remote by Charles was a big deal, earning you significant attention from the rest of the group, especially the girls.

Drama festivals were my favourite. Behind the drama festivals was Mr. Chirchir, a literature scholar known for his smart appearance, strength, good sense of humour, and honesty. His literature skills were top-notch. I vividly remember him teaching and summarising a set book by Chinua Achebe; in one memorable scene, a character fell in love and yelled out "Ralph," an ex-boyfriend, in a moment of passion. This scene left some classmates with their hands in their pockets, eagerly begging to hear more. Mr. Chirchir's unique teaching style and creativity made his classes unforgettable. His ability to bring literature to life was a gift, and he truly was a role model for all of us. I have always been a good actor, and being part of the drama team was exhilarating because it allowed us to intermingle with other big schools during competitions. It was also a ticket to free trips to local schools and, depending on our performance, potentially even bigger high schools. Although we didn't travel very far, we did participate in a few competitions at notable schools. These trips were fun not only because of the excitement of the bus ride but also because we were treated to a special lunch of soda and bread. It may sound funny, but that meal was a real treat, especially if you managed to get your favourite soda and perhaps an extra one if you were lucky. We always carried extra pocket money to buy our own snacks, adding to the enjoyment of these memorable trips.

I also liked sports, even though I could not play them. I was one of those students you would just want to take to competitions to socialise with others, make noise, and at the end of the day be exhausted from running up and down and screaming for a team that would definitely lose. I was also part of the medic team, and you would come to me in case of injuries or minor illnesses. Our team always lost in most of the sports because it was still a small school, and the selection of players was sometimes based on who was available to play the assigned game. We did not have enough resources, but as time went by, we started developing and getting equipped. The only event we never lost was the high jump. There was a guy named Hillary who was about 6 feet and a few inches tall who could jump, leaving everyone in awe. He was good, and I never saw him practice or warm up at all. His competition started at the nationals because no one else was at his level at the district and provincial levels. I understand his older siblings were also good at sports, but I never got to witness them during their time.

There were also school religious rallies held across neigh-bouring schools over the weekends, mostly on Sundays because most of us pray on Sundays. There was no transportation for these trips; they were not funded, and walking was approved by the school administration, which we liked. The furthest we went was to Tenwek High School, about 10 miles away. It was a whole-day trip but only for the serious ones who were inspired and wanted to make a change in their lives. The other reason for attending was to get other schools to attend our rally whenever we held one.

The most successful rally held by the Christian Union was during my leadership supervised by Christian Union Leader Mr. Mutai and the love of his life Emily. These two were inseparable; not even water could come between them. It was evident they were meant to be together, bonded by both spirit and law. He was a distinctive figure with his bald head and glasses that perched lightly on his nose, framing his thoughtful eyes. His most memorable features, however, were his two brown teeth that peeked out whenever he smiled—a smile that was always warm and welcoming. Despite his quiet demeanour, Mr. Mutai exuded a constant cheerfulness that brightened the atmosphere around him. He had a gentle presence, often found observing quietly yet attentively, ready to offer a kind word or a piece of advice. His demeanour was a comforting blend of wisdom and approachable friendliness, making him a beloved figure among those who knew him.

Following Mr. Mutai was an inspiring team of young leaders: Philemon, Festus, my younger brother, and Ruto. Ruto was a short, hard charger who was always impeccably clean and smelled good, dressing to impress with a spotless white shirt changed daily, shiny shoes, and a clean haircut, easily recognisable as the short, clean, smiling guy you couldn't miss. These dynamic individuals, driven by their motivation and enthusiasm, managed to rally over 300 members of the congregation on a bright Sunday afternoon for worship. Their leadership and passion created an electrifying atmosphere, bringing the community together in a powerful display of faith. A particularly memorable moment was when Pastor Kirui, the impeccably dressed and clean-cut faith church pastor, took the congregation to an even higher level with his infectious worship energy. His fervour and spirit were so compelling that they had everyone off their seats, singing and cheering for the Lord. This uplifting experience left a lasting impression on all who attended, showcasing the incredible impact of dedicated leadership and heartfelt worship.

We had a couple of schools show up, and most of the teachers, including the headteacher, attended. We called it a weekend challenge because it started on Friday night with a sermon, and teachings took place all Saturday, with the main concluding service on Sunday. In the main service, we made sure the schools that attended were well fed, seated, and given a chance to present a song and have their representative give a speech. At the end of the service, we escorted them and wished them well as they departed back to their respective schools. This courtesy made them feel at home and willing to come back again next time they were invited. These events required a lot of planning and execution skills and definitely a good leader to coordinate and ensure everything went as planned. To ensure the event's success, we planned ahead, usually at the beginning of the term, and started inviting guest speakers in advance to put them on the calendar.

Rono and Patrick were renowned cooks, widely respected for their culinary skills and dedication. These pioneers in the community were not only talented but also incredibly energetic, always going the extra mile to ensure everyone was well-fed. Their passion for cooking was evident in everything they did, and it was especially highlighted on Sundays when they prepared a cup of tea for over 300 members of the congregation. Despite the daunting task, Rono and Patrick approached it with enthusiasm and love, their cheerful spirits infusing warmth into every cup they served. Their dedication went beyond mere duty; it was a labor of love that reflected their commitment to the community and their joy in bringing people together through their delicious and comforting tea.

Another important figure behind the cooks was the Matron. According to Google's definition, her job involved acting as a role model and professional to support nurses and practitioners at all levels of patient care. In our school, she was tasked with leading and coordinating cleanliness standards across her areas of responsibility. Her presence around the school compound was unmistakable, with her round, gorgeous eyes, round body, and no-nonsense attitude. Despite her stern demeanour, she had a good sense of humour and always took care of business. One notable instance when she rose to the occasion was when a girl went unconscious due to a medical condition. Some of us thought the student might die, as it took about an hour to arrange transportation. A messenger had to seek help from the few individuals who had vehicles at that time. Renowned Edwin arap Rop saved the day by providing transportation on credit. The Matron truly earned her pay check that day by ensuring the student was breathing and providing support until the family arrived to take over. Working alongside the Matron was Susana, the quality assurance and safety personnel responsible for ensuring that the food was cooked to standard and met all requirements. However, she often found herself cooking instead of performing her official duties, frequently frustrated by the demands of the special diet students mentioned earlier.

Despite these challenges, Susana's hospitality was unquestionable, always going above and beyond to meet the needs of everyone.

I was in form three in the year 2003. This was the moment when I started realising that time was moving fast, and I was about to graduate from high school. I teamed up with a few friends, including my brother, who was in form two then, to start remedial studies during odd hours. We did not have electricity, but I had a lantern lamp as a gift. We got kerosene from the accountant, who we made sure to get along with very well. I knew him outside of class; he was our close family friend. We always made sure to do what he asked of us to get financed for kerosene throughout the term. It was expensive, and we consumed more than normal due to the extra time we put in after classes late at night or early in the morning. During school holidays and weekends, when everyone else was sleeping in, we would wake up at 3:00 a.m. and study like it was the end of the world. We did that repeatedly until we were discouraged by one of our teachers, concerned that it was too much, and we were exhausting our brains. It was then enforced that no one was to be awake after 10:00 p.m. or earlier than 5:00 a.m. We could not believe it and started getting smarter. We complied for the first few days but realised we were losing a lot of time and studying. So, we decided to start back again. We were hunted for the first few days by the watchman, ordering us to go to bed. We worked something out with him. We told him we would help look after the classrooms if he concentrated on the security of the other buildings. I guess it worked because he never bothered us again, and we kept on with our studies. That's why we performed better than the rest of the school.

The person behind our long hours of study was Bursar, an

accountant who, coincidentally, shared my name. Mr. Mutai, affectionately known as Bakarna, was exceptionally generous, often providing money for kerosene out of his own pocket. His dedication was truly inspiring. Even when we pestered him for funds and he sincerely had none to spare, he always found a way to make things happen. Bakarna's unwavering support ensured that we had the light we needed to study late into the night. His selflessness and commitment went beyond mere financial assistance; he became a beacon of hope and motivation for us all. His actions not only facilitated our education but also taught us the value of generosity and the importance of supporting each other in our academic endeavours.

On the security side, ensuring our safety was *Bamongo*, better known by his village name, *Cheram,* but his real name was Mr. Cheruiyot. His dedication to security was worthy of an Oscar award. This old man was vigilant throughout the night, aware of every activity that occurred in the school during those hours. Despite the long hours—12 hours a day, seven days a week—*Cheram* remained steadfast in his duties. Armed with his traditional bows and arrows, he was a formidable presence, and no intruder dared to breach the compound under his watch. His commitment and unyielding vigilance provided us with a sense of security and peace, allowing us to focus on our studies without fear. *Cheram's* tireless efforts and unassailable presence made him an indispensable guardian of our safety. *Cheram* was also known for his beautiful daughters, and I had a particular eye for one of them, Chepngeno, who I understand is now happily married. Her beauty was truly exceptional, with captivating eyes and a radiant smile that showcased her perfect teeth. At the time, I was too young to approach her directly, so my interactions with her were limited to brief moments as we passed each other on the road or the rare occasions when I heard her voice during visits to her sister Anna. Anna was married to my next-door neighbour, Paul, a man whose character is beyond description. Paul's boundless energy and strength were legendary, often requiring two men to handle him. Known for his farming prowess and his willingness to lend a helping hand during gatherings, Paul was the go-to person whenever a job needed to be done efficiently and effectively. His presence was a cornerstone of the community, embodying reliability and robust support.

It wasn't very long before my last year of high school approached. Academically, I was ranked third. This is called indexing. At the beginning of the term in form four, we had to sit for an exam that ranked students based on their performance. Index one was the first position, the second, and so forth. The same system was also common, emphasising that there was always room for improvement through hard work for everybody regardless of their index number. I liked most subjects except Math, Chemistry, and Swahili, but I had to put in all the effort for the sake of the National Exam, which was around the corner. I don't know who developed these kinds of exams because I always thought they were designed to mock students. You would find that the majority of those who sat for the exam were never satisfied.

I took the exam as a routine to graduate high school and to figure out a way forward afterwards, whether to go for post-secondary education or stay at home until further notice. Exams were administered in October and went on for a month and a few days. It was just exams one after the other and reviews for the upcoming papers. Most subjects comprised papers one and two, and I think this is why most people did not perform very well. It was too much information to hold on to, and the exam was cumulative, including everything covered in the last four years. Even now, with the level of knowledge I have, I still think it was too hard. But some students are smart enough to score for almost everything. I remember one of my classmates we nicknamed "lawyer" scored 99 percent in math when I struggled to score 60 percent. It was nearly impossible, and it was easy to score an E. Grades ranged from excellent (A) to poor (E), but you had to be really poor in class to score an E. It was still a grade but wouldn't take you anywhere. Some students in the district struggled with their academic performance, consistently scoring an E in all subjects. Occasionally, a few managed to obtain a D-minus, which, despite being slightly better, was still considered a poor grade as it essentially reflected simply writing one's name, filling in demographic information, and completing the entire test without demonstrating adequate subject knowledge. It was very easy. The grade was still good because most people wanted to know if you had achieved a high school diploma or not. In such cases, you would brag about graduating from 12th grade and claim you were not issued the diploma due to unpaid fees.

After the exams were completed, all the students were required to check out to be issued their school leaving certificates, which were simply letters of good conduct. The deputy headteacher, Mr. Kirui, well known for his bald head and impeccable dress code, was a distinguished physics teacher with over 20 years' experience. His reputation extended beyond the classroom, as he was also a trusted counsellor to many students. His dedication to discipline, cleanliness, and professional attire set a standard that inspired everyone around him. Mr. Kirui's teaching was not only about imparting knowledge but also about nurturing character and guiding his students towards their future endeavours. When I needed a letter of conduct, he wrote one for me, filled with genuine praise and encouragement, reflecting his belief in my potential. His kind words and well-wishes for my career journey were a testament to his commitment to his students' success, leaving a lasting impact on my life.

10

L ife at home after high school was not at all fun because I was now a grown-up. I was legally eighteen years of age, a registered voter, and I had many decisions to make, all requiring parental approval. Most people enjoyed life after high school, but not for long due to farm labor during their time at home. Most parents enjoyed this time because they got extra help, and you were always there when needed, even when the rest of the family was back at school. I think I was my father's favourite because we got along so well, and I did most of the tasks he assigned me, including going to the bank on his behalf to withdraw money. The local bank allowed an approved designated person to withdraw money on behalf of the account owner as part of customer service. I hated it because there was a lot of queuing for hours, listening to farmers complain about high tax cuts, low pay, long wait times to get served, and sometimes hunger, which no one cared about.

A break from going to school and having to study was totally fine for me, plus not seeing some faces at school and not being bothered was a relief. I did miss sitting in class in a uniform and doing school routines, which mostly involved hygiene and tea breaks. Tension started when the national exam results were around the corner. Everyone, including those who did not sit for the exam, constantly asked if the results had been announced, just to get on your nerves. This was a good time to avoid going to public places unless it was for official business-like shopping or going to church. This was also an excellent time to keep away from girls because you did not want to risk being responsible for anyone else's life.

When the results were announced, I was really nervous to check them at school. All the people I knew at school who seemed to know the results did not want to discuss them. To me, it was either bad news or a policy that did not allow them to tell you. The next morning, I toughened up and went to school to see the results for myself. I was satisfied to learn that I had scored a mean grade of C. I did not care what everyone else had scored because I knew I had worked hard for my grade and did not care what anyone else thought. This was also the most stressful and depressing moment because everyone, including those who knew nothing about grades, wanted to sit you down and plan your life. The most annoying thing was having someone tell me to enrol again in form four. I never appreciated it because high school was behind me, and I was set on other opportunities.

"C material" or "Charlie material" was a common term for those who scored such a grade. I was offered a job by one of my former teachers, but I turned it down, feeling it was a waste of time and not what I expected from a mentor who should push me towards greater achievements. This triggered a period of intense self-reflection and sleepless nights as I grappled with my next steps. External pressures were mounting—some of my close friends had scored well and were preparing to join public universities, while others, who didn't meet the cut-off points, were planning to retake the national exams. Many people advised me to do the same, but the ultimate decision rested with my sponsor, my father, and me. The situation was frustrating, but after sending out several college applications, I began to receive acceptance letters. This was a turning point, making me realise that despite my grade, I still had the potential to pursue something meaningful and carve out a future for myself.

I was motivated once again, and the first course I took was basic computer applications, essentially learning how to use a computer. It was 2005, and I had never used a computer before. Being a fast learner, I completed the course part-time in three months, mastering the basics without internet access. Many people around me, whom I had underestimated, were skeptical and never supported the idea of learning about computers. At that time, not many understood the importance of computer literacy or its potential benefits. The first computer-literate person I ever heard of was an older gentleman who proudly claimed his job involved computer work. Initially, I thought his entire job revolved around computers, but I later realised he was probably an accountant. Living in the village often felt like being on the dark side, disconnected from technological advancements that were transforming the world elsewhere. Despite the lack of support and understanding, I persevered, driven by the belief that acquiring computer skills would open up new opportunities and broaden my horizons.

I never owned a cell phone until mid-2006. I saved up to buy a second-hand one from a friend, named Stone. It was a

Nokia cell phone, one of those with a battery that could last up to a week. Its main purpose was to call, text, withdraw, or send money, and maybe play the snake game, but you wouldn't play it for too long for fear of draining the battery because it cost a few shillings to recharge. Only a few owned coloured-screen phones, dumb phones, because there was nothing like a smartphone back then. Blackberries were smartphones, but there was no way you could own one unless you were from the city or knew friends abroad who could send you one.

In late 2007, I began my first job as a volunteer elementary school teacher at a private school located about four miles from home. I took on the role during the holiday season when pupils were attending remedial classes.

I genuinely enjoyed teaching and dedicated three weeks to the job, including Saturdays. However, at the end of this period, we were sent home empty-handed, without any pay—not even enough for laundry soap. I was disgusted and felt a surge of anger at such a selfish act. Who offers a job without any form of compensation? It seemed unthinkable, yet it was the harsh reality we had to face. There was no recourse; taking the owner to court was out of the question since court fees were unaffordable, and there was always the fear that he had connections that could make things worse. This experience was a bitter reminder of the exploitation that was an unfortunate part of life, leaving me feeling helpless and betrayed.

I left the private school for another neighbouring school, deciding to send a child to collect my dues for me. After a few months, I was finally paid—it was only Ksh.500, equivalent to $3.89, but it was better than nothing and kept me going. My next job was at another private school, owned by the son of an old man who possessed a large piece of land. I hoped for better pay and conditions. While the job was good, the pay came in frustrating instalments. At the end of each month, we received only a fraction of our salary, with the rest trickling in later. This meant that over time, the pay started accumulating, creating a significant backlog if you stayed for a year or more. Realising the financial instability and the risks of remaining in such a situation, I decided not to take the chance. Instead, I ran off, encouraged by my neighbour, who was building another private school just about a hundred meters from my home. This new opportunity promised stability and proximity, making it a much more appealing option.

I took the chance and started my new job close to home; it took me five minutes to reach school compared to the other two, which took 45 minutes to an hour. It was a relief, and I started working, doing my farming at home at the end of the day and over the weekend. I began to like it. The owner was a retired agricultural officer, civilised, and knew how painful it was not to pay teachers. He made sure we got paid on time and for what we deserved. He was good, and besides, he was my relative, and life got better. I started making friends and socialising with the teachers I taught. We started to know each other and enjoyed the job. It was good, and it was the right decision. Together with the other four founding teachers, we motivated students to bring friends. We taught very well, and our students spoke national languages from preschool to fourth grade.

We keep up the good work. The school manager and his wife's generosity kept us motivated. We were now part of the family. Mr. and Mrs. Sigei were the embodiment of generosity and kindness. Their home was always open and welcoming. They treated me as one of their own, constantly encouraging me to aim higher and pursue my dreams. Mr. Sigei, with his infectious cheerfulness and warm smile, always found time to offer guidance and support, whether it was with schoolwork or life's challenges. Mrs. Sigei, equally good-hearted, was a nurturing presence, providing not just meals, but a sense of comfort and stability. Together, they created an environment where I felt valued and inspired. Their unwavering belief in my potential and their consistent words of encouragement fuelled my ambition, making me strive for excellence in everything I did. Their generosity extended beyond material things; they gave their time, their wisdom, and their love, ensuring I always felt supported and motivated to reach for the stars.

We turned their living room into our dining hall, sharing meals and conversations that bridged our lives. The family had two kids, and I overheard the oldest one expressing a desire to go abroad for further studies. For an elementary volunteer school teacher like me, who had scored a mean grade of C, the idea of studying abroad seemed like a distant dream—something reserved for wealthy tycoons who could afford the exorbitant costs of foreign education and plane tickets. It was almost unthinkable for someone from our background to aspire to such heights. However, my cousin offered to help my younger brother apply for a scholarship. Given that he had completed school, was eager to try, and there were no other siblings in high school at that time, we thought it was a great opportunity. This gesture ignited a spark of hope, challenging our preconceived notions of what was possible and opening the door to new possibilities for our family.

My brother had been gone for months. His activities in one of the local towns in *Juja* were a mystery to most, but I stayed in constant touch with him, gaining insight into his journey. Being computer literate, I was able to assist him with the intricacies of his tasks, such as emailing cross-country coaches, filling out online applications, and using visa cards. Our phone conversations were filled with jargon that sounded like code to anyone overhearing, yet it was simply the language of determination and ambition. Driven by a burning desire to leave the village and pursue a better life abroad, my brother meticulously navigated the complex process of securing a passport and an athletic scholarship, a journey that spanned six challenging months. By the seventh month, his hard work paid off, and he obtained a visa to attend Sheridan College in Wyoming, marking the beginning of a new chapter in his life.

Both my brother and my boss daughter Debbie left to begin their journey in the U.S. in January 2008, and we bid them goodbye and wished them the best. Everywhere there were those who believed in trying something new and those who mocked everything. This was different because no one had ever heard anyone in the entire village talking about going abroad for school unless they had a mean score of A plain, a grade that was nearly impossible to obtain. Less than 200 students in the entire country were able to attain the grade. In the whole district, there were only a few. That criterion alone made talking about going to the United States for further studies an impossible mission. It attracted attention from the neighbourhood, and we had some people visiting to discourage the idea of sending a kid abroad for studies because of so many beliefs. One would say so and so went and couldn't speak the vernacular when they returned; others said the kids would never recognise their parents when they got back, while others thought the kids would vanish into the air. It was a milestone, but my father stood firm. It was the toughest decision I had ever seen him make. He resisted all the forces trying to pull him and told whoever came home to let the kids do what they wanted. It was time we started seeing changes at home. Many things changed, and we were involved in decision-making and sharing ideas.

I was happy and felt like I was the one who got the scholarship. The news spread like wildfire in the village and the entire location. The day he came back from the city, you couldn't believe it. He was skinny and looked like he had some sort of deficiency in his diet, but after explaining how much he sacrificed, it all made sense. We planned a farewell for him together with the neighbour who introduced him to the idea. We rejoiced and started to see miracles happening, and above all, most mouths in the village were shut. They started to believe that everything was possible because the milestone of impossibility had been passed by just two people in the village. The farewell party was planned abruptly, and I still remember most people recommending more time and planning to invite guests of honour to do fundraising. My father said that everything was taken care of, and what was left was just to bid the student goodbye and give him words of advice.

The whole experience was a shock to many, as the common narrative was that only students from wealthy families, backed by millions of shillings, could afford to study abroad. In our case, it was quite the opposite. "How did you do it?" was the question on everyone's lips, and the answer was straightforward: applying for opportunities, following the correct procedures, and listening to the right advice. Above all, having the necessary resources was crucial. Before my brother's departure to the United States, I assisted him with his shopping for personal supplies and accompanied him to the airport. During this time, I also had the opportunity to meet his friends who were camping together in *Juja,* all engaged in the same process of applying for scholarships. These high school graduates were laid-back and friendly, and I quickly considered them family. They asked me when I would be joining them, and I confidently told them it wouldn't be long before I did. Their camaraderie and shared ambition were inspiring, and it felt like the beginning of a new chapter not just for my brother, but for all of us.

We later escorted my brother to the airport. He boarded British Airways and was required to be at the airport at 10:00 a.m. He did it and was gone, leaving me behind wondering if I could fit in his shoes. I knew I could, but it was just a matter of time to quit my volunteer job and begin this new journey of hope and better things. Nairobi CBD is chaotic at night, but my uncle Joel, son of *Kiboit*, was the mastermind behind navigating the traffic and ensuring my brother made it to the airport on time. His experience living in the city centre was unparalleled; he had an uncanny ability to make things happen. When he discovered that my brother's flight time was approaching and we needed to get him to the airport immediately, he made a quick phone call that lasted less than 30 seconds. In no time, a car pulled over, and the driver, well-versed in the city's maze of streets, expertly manoeuvred through the traffic. Within minutes, my brother was at the airport, ready to embark on his journey. Uncle Joel's resourcefulness and connections turned a potentially stressful situation into a seamless operation, showcasing his exceptional ability to manage the hustle and bustle of Nairobi with ease.

The day I got back home from the city, all the family were excited to hear that his travel plans were executed accordingly. Everything was new to us, and we did not need any extra help from experts. Many people offered to help, but we turned them down because we knew what we were doing.

Getting a plane ticket was something most people believed you needed to know somebody to bargain with or help with purchasing it. But this time, they were all wrong because my brother had everything paid off and was only required to show up at the airport with a passport and be ready to go. None of this information was known except for us. We had so much information that the most educated people around did not know what to ask for or how to help. By this time, I started getting a sense that everything was possible, and it was the right time to try my best.

11

Ben's and Debbie's journey to achieve their dreams served as powerful inspiration and a wake-up call, prompting me to reassess my own path. Although I loved spending time with the kids at school and mentoring them, I realized that I needed to mentor myself. Determined to change my course, I decided to leave my job and head to *Juja*, a place where I could train cross-country and make myself marketable for an athletics scholarship. Despite not being a natural runner, I was driven by the legacy of runners in my family. My uncle Philip often teased me about my tiny legs, annoyingly reminding me that they were meant for running. He wasn't entirely wrong; running talent runs in our family. My older sister Agnes could run so effortlessly it seemed her feet barely touched the ground. My older brother, a natural sprinter, often ran to impress, leaving the girls in awe during sports events. These family influences, combined with my father's unwavering ambition and love for education, which he never had the opportunity to pursue himself, fuelled my intense training and focus on running. I hoped to join a cross-country team overseas, driven by a desire to honour my family's legacy and my father's relentless push for us to reach our full potential.

In *Juja*, you meet people like Choge, Gideon, Roba, Tito, Walter, Victor who we always made fun of and Pentagon, among others—masterminds of creativity and unbeatable computer skills. These guys knew how to manoeuvre the digital world, making online payments and browsing the internet with impressive finesse. They had a unique gift for turning a mere Shs.5 into an hour of browsing, thanks to their charming ability to sweet-talk Fredy and Winny, a memorable couple who ran the local internet café. Fredy and Winny were incredibly supportive, often letting us browse on credit because they believed in our potential and wanted us to achieve our goals. If they could share all the stories, they would likely recount thousands of unpaid browsing debts, forgiven out of their genuine desire to help us succeed. Their kindness and belief in our dreams left a lasting impact, making them unforgettable figures on our journey towards a better future.

I spent about six months in *Juja* training and browsing in cybercafé, supported by peers who were also chasing their dreams. No time was wasted, and the positive influence around Jomo Kenyatta University of Agriculture and Technology (JKUAT) was inspiring. Watching scholars take taxis in the form of bicycles to attend their lectures always motivated us. At times, we imitated them and used university resources to our advantage, including water, TVs, and satellite phones. We even used their mailbox, which is where we met Mr. Kinyua, an administrator and the main mailman. Mr. Kinyua was nice when he was in a good mood but could be mean when he was in a bad one. To cut the story short, it was sometimes easy to tip him off by promising to send him some goodies once we went abroad. I remember promising him a Blackberry, a costly item at that time. Although I lost contact with him and never kept that promise, I still acknowledge his support and the role he played in our journey.

The living situation in *Juja* was harsh and crowded, with up to eight tenants crammed under the same roof in a space comparable to a small floor area. Our home had just one bed, a radio, and a stove for cooking. The number of cups and plates was minimal, reflecting the tiny size of our household. Our feeding schedule was a crucial aspect of our daily life, with each tenant taking turns feeding the rest for a full day. How you managed to come up with money for breakfast, lunch, and dinner was your own concern. Sometimes, if funds were short, you could borrow from someone or simply disappear, but vanishing would erode trust within the group, so every effort was made to meet the needs. To lift everyone's spirits, there was *Bite*, the renowned soup maker known for his delicious broths and stuffed cow's intestines, or *mutura*. This dish was a must-try, and a cup of his soup added to the Sukuma Wiki would earn you the crew's lasting appreciation and affection. Roba was the best ugali maker; his skill at preparing the staple left our taste buds salivating. Gideon, famous for his *Sukuma Wiki,* rounded out our culinary team. These boys had honed their skills well, often making our own culinary attempts seem amateurish in comparison. Their talents brought a sense of comfort and community to our challenging living conditions.

Tough living conditions and the constant need to ask my parents for financial support pushed me to my limits. Finally, I received an admission letter and an I-20 form, marking the beginning of my visa application process to join Fort Lewis

College, a public liberal arts college in Durango, Colorado. Fort Lewis has a unique history, transitioning from a military fort to an Indian boarding school, and eventually to a state public school. The masterminds behind my admission were Coach Ken Flint, a fine gentleman and a man of his word, who guided me through every step of the process until I became a team member. Another significant figure was Coach John Weswah, a hardworking individual known for always wearing his ball cap backwards, stating that there was no rule against it. Together, they pulled all the strings to ensure I was on the team and promised to keep the team shining. Additionally, Mike, a student at the time, provided unwavering support, answering my questions and teaching me essential survival skills, which I will detail in my next book. The combined efforts of these individuals were instrumental in my journey, and their support will never go unnoticed.

After completing all the required paperwork, it was time to visit the United States Embassy for my F-1 student visa interview. Uncle Joel, whom you might remember from my earlier descriptions, played a crucial role by leveraging his connections to help me gather some of the necessary financial statements. Another key figure was Buretti, an outgoing yet quiet gentleman who had worked with Kenya Commercial Bank since we were kids. Without hesitation, Buretti provided the essential documents I needed to meet interview expectations. I last met him at the Kencom building on the fifth floor —a tall man, impeccably dressed in a tie. His professional appearance and sponsorship filled me with confidence, making me feel overqualified for the visa interview. Their support was invaluable, and I walked into the embassy with a sense of assurance and readiness.

Choge Junior ensured I woke up on time for the big day at

the U.S. Embassy in *Gigiri*. Close friends, like Walter, wished me well as I arrived at my destination at 6:00 a.m. I was tense but reassured myself that I had done everything right. The sight of the General Service Unit at the compound and the restricted traffic on that route was a stark reminder of the high stakes. Most of the other guests with appointments at the same time appeared to be from the business class; their appearances spoke of wealth. My interview lasted about three minutes. I warmly greeted the interviewer, answered a few questions, and the last thing I remembered hearing was, "Congratulations and good luck with your education and athletics." That moment was surreal. I ran out, cheerful and ecstatic; anyone who saw my face could tell I had succeeded. Outside the gate, I made a few phone calls to my parents and friends, sharing the good news. They gladly received it, and I knew that another chapter in my life was about to begin.

I communicated the exciting news to Coach Flint, who provided me with the anticipated arrival time. I went ahead and booked my flight. At this moment, that little boy from the village was preparing to travel for further studies at a college in Colorado—an institution that costs over two million Kenyan shillings a year. Unbelievable, right? My confidence soared; I felt unstoppable and could enter any government office or building without hesitation. This newfound confidence boosted my belief in my potential. After a few chats with my father, he miraculously wired me the ticket money. To this day, I'm unsure how he managed to come up with KSh.110,000, about $1,200 at the time, on such short notice. With the funds in hand, I proceeded to Qatar Airways headquarters and purchased my ticket. I then traveled home to bid my family goodbye, ready to embark on this incredible new chapter in my life.

Arriving home, I sensed that my status quo had changed; friends saw me differently, though my character and personality remained the same. Seeing my father's smile and the love in his eyes, knowing that his blessings had come to pass, was deeply inspiring. We had a long conversation where he shared how our family had prayed continuously for our success. The hug and handshake we exchanged felt like a man-to-man acknowledgment, filled with confidence that change was on the horizon. My mother, on the other hand, had tears rolling down her cheeks—a sign of profound relief and joy. I couldn't imagine the heartbreak of returning home empty-handed, but seeing their pride and happiness affirmed that I had made them proud.

The village organised a heartfelt farewell, a tradition to wish students well as they embarked on their journeys to chase their dreams. The Sigei family played a crucial role, providing a facility to host about 200 people. Motivational speakers graced the event, including *Bomor* and the late Chief Kosgei, who was a close mentor, along with Richard Kosgei, both always keen on the neighbours' academic progress. Various church leaders led a powerful prayer session, surrounding me with their blessings and invoking angels to guide and protect me. This send-off was not just a personal milestone; it symbolised hope, transformation, and inspiration for other students in the neighbourhood, encouraging them to pursue their own dreams.

The day I bid farewell to the Valley View Academy kids was a whirlwind of emotions, filled with laughter, excitement, and a touch of sadness. The schoolyard buzzed with energy as classmates and teachers gathered around, their faces beaming with pride and joy. My friends, who had been by my side through thick and thin, enveloped me in tight hugs, their eyes sparkling with excitement for my journey to the United States. We took countless photos, capturing these precious moments of camaraderie and celebration. Amidst the cheerful chaos, heartfelt goodbyes were exchanged, with promises to stay in touch and continue supporting each other from afar. Teachers offered words of wisdom and encouragement, their voices filled with hope and pride. As I climbed into the car, ready to embark on this new adventure, I waved one last time, my heart full of gratitude for the love and support of the Valley View Academy community. Their cheers and well-wishes echoed in my ears, a reassuring chorus that would accompany me on my journey across the ocean.

As the evening shadows lengthened, casting a warm, golden hue over the familiar landscapes of my village, I stood surrounded by the people who had been my world. Family, friends, and villagers gathered, their faces etched with a mix of pride, disbelief, and bittersweet smiles. My never-aging cousin Renson stood beside me, his reassuring presence a constant source of strength. The reality of my departure felt surreal; at 23, I was about to embark on a journey that seemed like a dream to everyone here—a Boeing Jet 737 awaited to carry me to Durango, Colorado. The weight of their expectations and dreams pressed gently on my heart as I hugged my parents tightly, their eyes glistening with unspoken words. With Renson's steady hand on my shoulder, we made our way to the car, every step echoing with the promises of a future unknown. As the car pulled away, I looked back one last time, the village fading into the twilight, knowing this was not just a goodbye, but the start of an incredible, unimaginable adventure that lay ahead.

After a series of airport security checks, I boarded the flight with a mix of excitement and fear, hardly believing that

I was finally on my way to a foreign country to begin my career journey and achieve my dream. Nervousness crept in as stories of flying flashed through my memory. Looking around, I noticed that not many passengers were of my age or background; most were foreigners returning to their countries. This starkly reminded me that I was leaving home, stepping into independence, and it was now up to me to make good decisions and navigate this new chapter in my life on my own. As the plane taxied down the runway, my heart raced with a mix of nervousness and exhilaration. The roar of the engines grew louder, and I felt a rush of anticipation. For a student from a poor background, flying to the United States for studies was a magical journey, a dream come true.

As the plane lifted off the ground, I pressed my face against the window, watching the city of Nairobi slowly shrink beneath me. The buildings and streets became tiny dots, and the familiar landscape faded away. My excitement mingled with a sense of awe and disbelief—I was really doing this, leaving home for a new world of opportunities. Alongside the thrill, there was poignant uncertainty about when I would return, adding a layer of bittersweet emotion to the moment. The realisation of my journey set in, filling me with hope and determination as I soared higher into the sky, ready to embrace the challenges and adventures that lay ahead, yet deeply aware of the ties I was temporarily severing.

THE END